Modern Critical Views

Edward Albee
Maya Angelou
Asian-American
 Writers
Margaret Atwood
Jane Austen
James Baldwin
Samuel Beckett
Saul Bellow
The Bible
William Blake
Jorge Luis Borges
Ray Bradbury
The Brontës
Gwendolyn Brooks
Robert Browning
Italo Calvino
Albert Camus
Lewis Carroll
Willa Cather
Cervantes
Geoffrey Chaucer
Anton Chekhov
Kate Chopin
Agatha Christie
Samuel Taylor
 Coleridge
Joseph Conrad
Contemporary Poets
Stephen Crane
Dante
Daniel Defoe
Charles Dickens
Emily Dickinson
John Donne and the
 17th-Century
 Poets
Fyodor Dostoevsky
W. E. B. Du Bois
George Eliot
T. S. Eliot
Ralph Ellison
Ralph Waldo
 Emerson
William Faulkner
F. Scott Fitzgerald

Sigmund Freud
Robert Frost
George Gordon,
 Lord Byron
Graham Greene
Thomas Hardy
Nathaniel
 Hawthorne
Ernest Hemingway
Hispanic-American
 Writers
Homer
Langston Hughes
Zora Neale Hurston
Henrik Ibsen
John Irving
Henry James
James Joyce
Franz Kafka
John Keats
Jamaica Kincaid
Stephen King
Rudyard Kipling
D. H. Lawrence
Ursula K. Le Guin
Sinclair Lewis
Bernard Malamud
Christopher Marlowe
Gabriel García
 Márquez
Carson McCullers
Herman Melville
Arthur Miller
John Milton
Toni Morrison
Native-American
 Writers
Joyce Carol Oates
Flannery O'Connor
Eugene O'Neill
George Orwell
Sylvia Plath
Edgar Allan Poe
Katherine Anne
 Porter
J. D. Salinger

Jean-Paul Sartre
William Shakespeare:
 Histories and
 Poems
William Shakespeare's
 Romances
William Shakespeare:
 The Comedies
William Shakespeare:
 The Tragedies
George Bernard
 Shaw
Mary Wollstonecraft
 Shelley
Percy Bysshe Shelley
Alexander
 Solzhenitsyn
Sophocles
John Steinbeck
Tom Stoppard
Jonathan Swift
Amy Tan
Alfred, Lord
 Tennyson
Henry David
 Thoreau
J. R. R. Tolkien
Leo Tolstoy
Mark Twain
John Updike
Kurt Vonnegut
Alice Walker
Robert Penn Warren
Eudora Welty
Edith Wharton
Walt Whitman
Oscar Wilde
Tennessee Williams
Thomas Wolfe
Tom Wolfe
Virginia Woolf
William Wordsworth
Richard Wright
William Butler Yeats

31.41

Contents

10 9 8 7 6 5 4 3 2 1

∞ The paper used in this publication meets the minimum
requirements of the American National Standard for
Permanence of Paper for Printed Library Materials,
Z39.48-1984

Library of Congress Cataloging-in-Publication Data
applied for

ISBN 0-7910-5921-9

Chelsea House Publishers
1974 Sproul Road, Suite 400
Broomall, PA 19008-0914

The Chelsea House World Wide Web address is
http://www.chelseahouse.com

Contributing Editor: Aaron Tillman

Produced by: Publisher's Services, Santa Barbara, California

Modern Critical Views

AGATHA CHRISTIE

Edited and with an introduction by
Harold Bloom
Sterling Professor of the Humanities
Yale University

CHELSEA HOUSE PUBLISHERS
Philadelphia

Editor's Note

This book brings together nine useful essays upon Agatha Christie's fiction, as well as an instance of her own self-reflection.

My Introduction meditates upon *The Murder of Roger Ackroyd*, and briefly considers the problematics of guilt in Christie's work.

G. C. Ramsey begins the chronological sequence of essays with a general survey of Christie's career, while Elizabeth Walter completes the survey of Christie's achievement in detective fiction.

Another Agatha Christie, who wrote under the name of Mary West-macott, was a writer of "unmystery novels" and is the subject of Dorothy B. Hughes' essay, after which Christie herself is heard from in her *Autobiography*, recounting the years of childhood and youth.

Julian Symons, poet and mystery writer, celebrates Christie as a "master conjurer," while Pam McAllister invokes gender differences to help account for the rival modes of Christie and of Raymond Chandler.

Robert Barnard attempts to defend Christie's craft, if not her art, after which Charles Osborne chronicles the interplay of Christie's career and her mysterious "disappearance" of 1926.

In another defense of Christie, Gillian Gill commends the author's supposed detachedness, while Anne Hart concludes the volume by centering upon the career of Hercule Poirot.

Introduction

"Who Cares Who Killed Roger Ackroyd?" is the title of a celebrated essay by Edmund Wilson, a strong critic who did not like detective fiction. The popular evidence (though not the literary) is against Wilson. Christie's books have sold well over a billion copies in English, and about the same number in 44 other languages. Only the Bible and William Shakespeare have more readers than Agatha Christie. Clearly, Christie's astonishing and universal popularity far transcends any intrinsic interest her books possess.

The genre of murder mysteries owes something to Poe, more to Conan Doyle, and has become a cosmos of print throughout the century now ending. Greatest of all detective novels, Dostoevsky's *Crime and Punishment* has unsurpassable elements in it, mysteries not to be solved. We never really learn why Raskolnikov became a murderer, and why he could not repent, until the book's "Epilogue." Christie in comparison has no mysteries: the lucid Poirot clarifies everything. But though Christie never achieves art (in my judgment), her craft is almost always considerable. She always knows what she is doing, perhaps indeed knows too well. Romance, literary and human, always is founded upon incomplete knowledge, and detective fiction is a late child of the ancient literary kind called romance.

I have just reread *The Murder of Roger Ackroyd* (1926), after about forty years. It remains briskly readable, and is ingeniously plotted. Hercule Poirot I resist; he is a taste I never acquired. Christie, in her book's dedication, describes it as "an orthodox detective story, murder, inquest, and suspicion falling on every one in turn!" Let us center upon that word, "orthodox," for there Christie gives us a clue to her craft. There is a displaced religiousity in murder mysteries: in *Crime and Punishment* of course no displacement exists. The fascination of the genre is more spiritual than it is literary.

The poet-critic W. H. Auden saw this very plainly when he emphasized that, as readers, we are relieved to discover that we at least are innocent, at the end of the story. "Guilt is never to be doubted," the motto of Kafka's "In the Penal Colony," is the repressed fear of every reader. Christie shrewdly builds upon this as suspicion progresses to everyone in turn, until at last the narrator concludes the book in the brief "Apologia" that confesses his own culpability.

Dr. Sheppard, the murderer-narrator, reads more impressively the second time around. Forty years ago, he seemed to me entirely too dry, but now he is the only interesting character in the book, Poirot included. The dryness conceals not well-bred malice, but something that approximates nihilism. Christie is not exactly Dostoevsky, and no one ever will mistake Dr. Sheppard for Svidrigailov or Stavrogin. "As a professional man, I naturally aim at discretion," Dr. Sheppard tells us at the start, and his silences are the most eloquent part of him. Christie tells us that he murdered initially to cover up blackmail, and then murdered to cover up murder. And yet Christie implies that Dr. Sheppard kills as a reflex of his own nature: his guilt is never to be doubted, least of all by himself, though his craft as narrator is to admit nothing until the end.

Nothing in Christie is actually plausible because, for her, contrivance is all. That is part of her skill, but only part. Her largest power is whole-heartedness as a plotter, and so Dr. Sheppard, like all her murderers, is her true surrogate. Hercule Poirot and Miss Marple are merely ideograms: Christie's endless success is the ability to enjoy her own guilt.

G. C. RAMSEY

The Career of Agatha Christie Mallowan

Agatha Christie finds it hard to be specific about just how she creates the plots which consistently baffle her readers. To a certain extent, it is difficult for any naturally talented person to explain how he comes by his talent. He soon learns the folly of saying "I don't know—it's just *easy*." For it is easy for a musician with perfect pitch to recognise a 440 A every time that he hears one, but very difficult for him to explain just why or how he can recognise and identify the sound so easily. Well-coordinated athletes are hard put to it to explain why they are good at tennis or golf, and as yet psychology has not been able to take the creative process in the arts and separate it into all of its component parts. It may, in fact, be that creativity is a gift, or a talent, as that latter word is used symbolically in the New Testament.

Not unnaturally, those who have been interested in the creative talent which Agatha Christie displays have sought some clue from her childhood. But here, Mrs. Christie maintains, they have been somewhat misled in that they have compared her background with that of a child brought up in the mid-twentieth century. By mid-twentieth-century standards, she had an unusually solitary childhood. She was the second daughter of an Anglo-American marriage, and her father, the American, died when she was little. Nigel Dennis in his *Life Magazine* article about Agatha Christie (1956), implies that Mrs. Miller (Agatha's mother) tutored Agatha at home. In this

From *Agatha Christie: Mistress of Mystery.* © 1967 by Dodd, Mead & Company.

day and age of super-organised activity for children, Mrs. Miller's actions would seem to many to be the height of cruelty, but it is well worth remembering that the American child who is whisked from school to ballet class to little league baseball to clarinet lessons never has a chance to learn to do anything really well. In an age when we have confused meditation with idleness, the idea of leaving a child alone with a book, or just alone to think, seems almost sacrilegious.

However, Mrs. Christie suggests that even in the period from 1890 to 1905 children were not quite so idle as we might conclude today from the fact that they were not sent out to school. She says, "At that time, girls very rarely went to school—it would have been thought a very odd thing to do! My elder sister, who was sent to 'the Miss Lawences at Brighton'—a pioneer school (afterwards Roedean)—created great surprise that Mr. and Mrs. Miller should have done such an extraordinary thing! All my friends had first a nurse or nursery maid, a nursery governess—later a governess or foreign nursery governess or sewing maid, more to look after or companion a child than to teach. As education, one had 'classes.' You went to Dancing Class— Swedish Exercises—Art School—Piano Lessons—Singing Class—Cookery Classes, etc. All I escaped was a resident governess—and certainly my mother was much better fun."

Yet the young Agatha Miller did have the time to investigate books and develop a liking for romance, fairy stories, Dickens, and Sherlock Holmes. Two events seem to stand out in her mind as high-water marks or influential moments—the first when she was ill in bed one time and her mother encouraged her to write a short story, which she did and found she enjoyed. The second event occurred about 1915, when her elder sister made a remark which surely must rank along with the challenge given Mary Shelley at dinner one night. In Mary Shelley's case, someone said that horror stories were difficult to do, and Mrs. Shelley (so the legend goes) rose to the occasion and said that she'd do one on a bet. Dr. Frankenstein and his nameless monster were the result of the challenge, and few people would dare to suggest that Mrs. Shelley did not win the bet hands down. Agatha Christie's sister said simply, "I bet you can't write a good detective story." It was a fortunate and stimulating challenge. For one thing, Agatha Christie had been writing up to that time "stories of unrelieved gloom, in which most of the characters died," according to her own admission. Secondly, having taken First Aid and Home Nursing Certificates, she joined a Voluntary Aid Detachment and worked in the Red Cross Hospital on the outbreak of the 1914 War, first as a nurse and then as a dispenser. (Her experiences along this line are suggested in *The Mysterious Affair at Styles*.) She gained from this work, in addition to a feeling of holy terror for the sisters in authority, a very good working knowledge of poisons, as the following poem, entitled "In a Dispensary," suggests. The poem comes from a privately printed collection entitled *Road of Dreams*, published in the early 1920's by Geoffrey Bles of London. Unfortunately, no American edition has ever existed.

IN A DISPENSARY

Oh! who shall say where Romance is, if Romance is not here?
For here are Colour, Death and Sleep . . . and Magic
everywhere!

Glistening salts, and shimmering scales, and crystals of purest
white,
High on the shelves in their spotless rows, enclosed in their
bottles bright,
Salts of iron of palest green, or deepening down to brown,
And many a tincture, many a wine, from far off lands
unknown . . .

Light as a promise, and bitter as sin—that feathery foam,
Quinine
And sedate beside it, in silver and black, the sea-born Iodine;
Soon shall it merge to orange and brown in a rich and
widening hue
Which perchance, in far-off Tyrian days, the old Phoenicians
knew.

Here heavy syrups, thick and sweet, prepared with skill and
toil,
And there, distilled in precious drops, stands many a spicèd
oil:
Lavender, Nutmeg and Sandalwood; Cinnamon, Clove and
Pine,
While above, in palest primrose hue, the Flowers of Sulphur
shine.

And high on the wall, beneath lock and key, the powers of the
Quick and Dead!
Little low bottles of blue and green, *each with a legend red.*
In the depths beneath their slender necks, there is Romance,
and to spare!
Oh! who shall say where Romance is, if Romance is not here?

From the Borgia's time to the present day, their power has
    been proved and tried!
Monkshood blue, called Aconite, and the deadly cyanide!
Here is sleep and solace and soothing of pain—courage and
    vigour new!
Here is menace and murder and sudden death!—in these
    phials of green and blue!

Here are copper salts that shame the heavens, and sparkle
    deep and blue,
And never a Mediterranean Sea shall match their Sapphire
    hue!
And oh! the many dazzling dyes—the golden-hued Flavine,
And the fine bronze dust that shall turn at will to a glory of
    Brilliant Green!

A philtre of Love—a philtre of Death—were they only a
    Sorcerer's lore?
To catch the pence, and trap the fool? Or were they some-
    thing more?
Beware of the Powers that never die, though Men may go
    their way,
The Power of the Drug, for good or ill, shall it ever pass
    away?

Oh! who shall say where Romance is, if Romance is not here?
For here are Colour, Death and Sleep . . . and Magic everywhere!

While Agatha Christie was working at the Red Cross Hospital in
Torquay, she had a chance to observe more than poisons. England was at the
time engaged in the resettlement of Belgian refugees, and a group of these
people were billeted near Torquay.

Agatha Christie was not the only writer aspiring to carry on the torch
lighted by Conan Doyle. In this country, for example, Robert Barr looked
around for an eccentric detective to lend character to his stories, and he
seized upon the idea of a retired French detective of enormous ego, whom
he christened Eugène Valmont, and who appeared in a short story collection
by Mr. Barr entitled (modestly) *The Triumphs of Eugène Valmont*. Agatha
Christie, working, as it turns out, quite independently, ten years later,
conceived of the idea of a retired foreign detective of superhuman ego who
would lend an exotic air to London. She chose the nearest thing at hand—

one of the Belgian refugees, and how Hercule Poirot, lately retired from the Brussels police force, came to England is detailed in *Styles*. Mrs. Christie readily acknowledges her debt to Conan Doyle, but says that she knew of Barr's work and was rather unimpressed by it. She preferred, she says, "the Sherlock Holmes form of construction, i.e., detective with idiosyncrasies and also with respectable, nice, but idiotic friend" The "idiotic friend" referred to is of course Capt. Arthur Hastings, whom Howard Haycraft has called "easily the stupidest of the modern Watsons." Mrs. Christie evidently tired of him, for she banished him to the Argentine in the late 1930's.

Armed, then, with her love of Sherlock Holmes and of storytelling, her working knowledge of poisons, and her casual acquaintance with the nearby Belgian refugees ("I doubt if I ever actually met any of them!" Mrs. Christie confides), Agatha Christie set out to meet her sister's challenge. *The Mysterious Affair at Styles* was promptly rejected by the first six publishers that saw it, but finally John Lane of the Bodley Head in London decided to take a gamble and publish it. His gamble paid off handsomely, and the writer Sutherland Scott has dubbed the book "one of the finest firsts ever written."

Although she says that she did not seriously consider making a living out of writing until she had sold five or six books, Agatha Christie did derive a good deal of pleasure and a not inconsiderable remuneration during the early 1920's from her writing, as her books came out at about the rate of one a year. She and her husband christened their house at Sunningdale, Berkshire, "Styles" after the success of the first novel, and Agatha Christie expressed much delight at owning her first car—a bottle-nosed Morris. She had become engaged some years previously, in 1912, to Archibald Christie, whom she married in 1914. She had joined the Voluntary Aid Detachment when he was sent on active duty in France as a Colonel in the Royal Flying Corps, and they had been reunited at the close of the war. All seemed to be going smoothly in 1926 when *The Murder of Roger Ackroyd* appeared. At this point, the detective story was still an even newer and more untried form than it is today, and Mrs. Christie simply thought up the idea of having one of the central characters hitherto considered above suspicion turn out to be the murderer. The detective world was rent in twain, with people crying "Foul!" and others, such as the mystery novelist Dorothy Sayers, crying "Fair! and Fooled you!"

Hard on the heels of this, Agatha Christie's mother died, and Agatha Christie sensed the impending breakup of her own marriage. These two pressures, together with the strain of constant work, became too much for her inventive mind to absorb all at once, and it revolted in one of the curious ways that minds have to relieve anxiety. Agatha Christie suffered an attack of amnesia, and simply walked out of her life one afternoon in 1926, abandoning her car in a field.

The amnesia has since been verified beyond any shadow of a doubt as genuine, but at the time there were doubts indeed among the general public. An anonymous tip led police to a hotel in Harrogate, Yorkshire, where a young lady was staying under an assumed name. The young lady, who was reported as being eager to play piano in trios with the orchestra there, turned out to be Agatha Christie, registered under the name of the woman who later became Colonel Christie's second wife.

What stung Mrs. Christie most about the whole unfortunate incident was that the press had accused her of disappearing as a publicity stunt to advertise her books, although why in the name of heaven she would have registered under the name she did if it were a publicity stunt never seemed to occur to people at the time.

It is a sad fact of life that the British press has been known upon occasion to be very cruel to famous people—American actresses constantly object to having the less happy aspects of their past pointed out to them in print as soon as they arrive in London.

To a certain extent, Mrs. Christie's desire for privacy has only fanned the flames of curiosity since 1926. For many years she sought to avoid any publicity whatsoever, and would not even let her publishers print her portrait with her books. She has said on numerous occasions that she feels authors (unlike actresses) ought to remain "background, shadowy figures," and, considering her unfortunate experience with publicity in 1926, one can certainly sympathise with her. Furthermore, some journalists (including those on a prominent Paris weekly) have resorted from time to time to tele-photo lenses to take pictures of Mrs. Christie as she sits eating in a restaurant, or as she comes out of one of her houses. Anyone who has ever had candid photos snapped of him unawares knows that most often the results are considerably less than flattering, and Mrs. Christie feels most decidedly that the pictures in question of her are that.

However, with the passing of time, Mrs. Christie has mellowed her views to the extent that she will grant interviews to responsible journalists who have the good taste to present their credentials to her agents and arrange for a mutually convenient interview—Nigel Dennis, Francis Wyndham, and the present author are three cases in point. For Mrs. Christie is very grateful for the affection and admiration in which she is held by her readers, and is not aloof but shy, as she suggests in her 1946 autobiographical *Come, Tell Me How You Live*.

Mrs. Christie divorced Col. Archibald Christie in 1928; he died in 1962. By this marriage she had a daughter, Rosalind, who, she says, "is my severest critic—and guesses the outcome of all my plots." On a holiday in Mesopotamia in 1930, she met Max Mallowan, archaeologist on the expedition led by Sir Leonard Woolley to reconstruct the ancient Sumerian city of Ur. She and Professor Mallowan were married in September 1930, and have lived very happily ever since.

Mrs. Christie (for she has kept this as her professional name) has never been one for letting good experience or knowledge go to waste. For many years she accompanied professor Mallowan on his excursions to the Middle East, and used the settings as background for several of what she calls her "foreign travel books"—*Death on the Nile, Murder in Mesopotamia,* and *Appointment with Death* are but three examples. Nor has she confined herself to the goings-on in the Middle East: she considers the getting there to be worthy of note as well, and satisfies the romantic wanderlust of her readers by chronicling train journies across Europe and the Middle East—*The Mystery of the Blue Train* and *Murder on the Orient Express* come immediately to mind, although the reader who wishes to read all the novels in a certain category can make up his own complete list from the material given in Appendix B.

During the Second World War, Mrs. Christie again worked in a dispensary, this time in London in University College Hospital. Her husband, Professor Mallowan, had joined the Royal Air Force, but was "seconded," or loaned out, by that organisation to the British Military government in North Africa to act as Advisor on Arab Affairs in Tripolitania. As Mrs. Christie said in her interview in the London *Sunday Times* with Francis Wyndham, there was little to do evenings during the war except write, and the war years showed the production of two of her most ingenious books, *The Labours of Hercules,* in which M. Poirot takes twelve cases to provide mental counterparts for his namesake's physical tasks, and *Death Comes as the End,* a *tour de force* set in Egypt in 2000 B.C., which required, as Mrs. Christie has said, "endless research on everyday details." In addition, these years produced the two posthumous novels, one a Poirot and the other a Miss Marple which will appear as the last books in their respective series as a sad farewell—we hope not for a good many years.

The Mallowans own at present two houses—Greenway House in Devonshire (pictured in the illustrations in this book); Winterbrook House, a smaller residence near Oxford; and they have a small flat in Chelsea for the occasions when they come up to London. Mrs. Mallowan in person is a large woman who gives the impression of being quite tall. She wears her grey hair pulled into an enormous French knot at the back of her head, and her blue eyes sparkle from behind her glasses. She still has a rather high soprano voice (she took singing lessons in Paris during her teens) and is quite shrewd and alert. The sense of humour which enlivens her books is apparent from her conversation, and she keeps up her interests in music and cooking. Her husband's book *Nimrud and Its Remains*, the culmination of thirty-five years' research in the Middle East, is dedicated to her and together with Mrs. Mallowan's own *Come, Tell Me How You Live*, provides a delightful (and colourful) insight into a shared career.

Two mistakes which have been perpetuated ought to be rectified. There have been, in fact, factual inaccuracies in articles about Mrs. Christie for years, and they are copied and recopied to the extent that it would almost be easier to change the facts to fit the fictions, and the present author is as guilty as anyone. It would be a great help to scholarship if all editors would checks their facts with Hughes Massie, Mrs. Christie's agents, before assuming anything to be true, and certainly before copying anything out of a previously published article. For instance, if we must know the date of Mrs. Christie's birth for library cards, it is 1890, and not 1891, in spite of all the library cards to the contrary; and the wrong date in fact appeared in my own article "Perdurable Agatha" in *The New York Times Book Review* in November 1965. Furthermore, the remark attributed to Mrs. Christie that "the older you get, the more interesting you become to an archaeologist" was the creation of some pundit whose neck Mrs. Christie would be glad to wring if he would care to identify himself—she neither made the remark nor does she consider it particularly complimentary or amusing.

But in spite of all the inaccuracies and invasions of privacy, Mrs. Christie looks back upon the first half century of her career with fondness and affection for her readers, although she admits to being a little awed at the idea that she must produce a Christie for Christmas each year lest the earth veer off its course. "A sausage machine, a perfect sausage machine," she calls herself.

But then, as she re-reads some of her favourite mystery authors and spots a trick she likes, she closes the book with a twinkle in her eye and says, "You know, it would be rather fun if I could do that. . . ."

ELIZABETH WALTER

The Case of the Escalating Sales

On 27 May 1926, two weeks after the end of the General Strike, when England was thankfully returning to normal and one or two of the fore-thoughtful were wondering if it would be worth saving for posterity copies of Churchill's emergency *British Gazette*, an event of more enduring literary significance occurred: *The Murder of Roger Ackroyd* was published.

It was not Agatha Christie's first novel, but it was the one which made her name, for the audacious ingenuity of its ending had critics and public divided on the issue of 'Was it fair?' It was also the first of her books to be published by Collins, and marked the beginning of an author–publisher relationship which endured for fifty years and well over seventy books.

When in the 1920s Sir Godfrey Collins and his editorial director, Mr F. T. Smith, began to build up a trade list in London for what had hitherto been a Glasgow-based publishing house chiefly distinguished for Bibles, educational books and the Collins Classics, they included among their early acquisitions a number of detective novels by authors such as Freeman Wills Crofts, G. D. H. Cole, Philip Macdonald, and others less well remembered. They sold satisfactorily. The up-and-coming publishers were therefore delighted when the literary agents Hughes Massie approached them with a script by Agatha Christie, an up-and-coming author who was already published by John Lane (Bodley Head). The script was so good that Collins

From *Agatha Christie: First Lady of Crime*. © 1977 by Holt, Rinehart and Winston.

11

eagerly entered into a three-book contract dated 27 January 1924, even though there were two books still to come from the Bodley Head. Two years later, *The Murder of Roger Ackroyd* was published at 7s 6d.

The thirty-four-year-old Mrs Christie was not an unknown quantity. Her first book, *The Mysterious Affair at Styles*, featuring a little Belgian detective named Hercule Poirot, had sold a mere 2,000 copies, but she was also well known as a writer of detective short stories. In 1923, when the weekly *Sketch* published a series of them, a whole page of pictures was devoted to the author at home, at her typewriter, on the telephone, or with her small daughter. Hughes Massie, her agents then as now, thought that Collins with their accent on detective fiction would be the ideal publisher in Britain. They were proved right. *The Murder of Roger Ackroyd* was published in a first edition of approximately 5,500 copies, and rapidly sold over 4,000 of these—considered then a very good sale. In America Agatha Christie was published from the first by Dodd, Mead.

Perhaps emboldened by this, Collins were able to make the following claim for their crime fiction in their catalogue for autumn 1926: 'We realize that the success of a Detective Novel depends upon the ingenuity and infallible accuracy of the author in the handling of his plot. We realize, too, that mere sensation based on irrelevant episodes will never make a good detective novel. We have accordingly set a very high standard. Only the best will do. That is why we have today the finest list of Detective Novels in existence.'

Despite the furor caused by *The Murder of Roger Ackroyd*, there was no reprint during the first year of publication, and the days when first printings would be ten times that initial figure were still far ahead. But a few months after publication an event occurred which was to have a profound—though not entirely favourable—effect on Agatha Christie's future career. She disappeared.

Suddenly the missing mystery writer was headline news, her name known throughout the country. Inevitably, there were those who said—unfairly—that it was a publicity stunt. Equally unfairly, there is no denying that the disappearance did indeed have a considerable effect on the sales of her next books. *The Big Four* (1927), which is really a collection of four linked short stories, sold over 8,500. *The Mystery of the Blue Train* (1928), based on a short story entitled 'The Mystery of the Plymouth Express' and described by Agatha Christie herself as 'easily the worst book I ever wrote', dropped to just below 7,000. *The Seven Dials Mystery* (1929), a sequel to an earlier book, *The Secret of Chimneys*, neither of them typical Christie, rose again to over 8,000. There can be few better examples of the effect of press publicity. Its ethics are another matter.

The year 1930 was a momentous one both for Agatha Christie person-ally and for the house of Collins. In September Mrs Christie, by now divorced, married the archaeologist Max Mallowan and began a life of great personal happiness. As if in celebration, the same year saw the publication of *Murder at the Vicarage*, the first book under a new six-book contract with Collins, in which Miss Jane Marple was introduced. For Collins, 1930 saw the birth of the Crime Club, the brainchild of Sir Godfrey and his nephew, young William Collins, who felt that the vogue for the detective story and the enormous popularity of book clubs could profitably be linked. Not that the Crime Club was ever a book club; simply the imprint under which Collins publish crime fiction. The first title was *The Noose* by Philip Macdonald, with a first printing of approximately 5,500. A few months later came *Murder at the Vicarage*. But by now the publicity bonanza was over and the first printing was back to 5,500. Agatha Christie did not shoot to best-sellerdom overnight.

It was not until *Three Act Tragedy* in 1935 (*Murder in Three Acts* in America) that she managed to sell 10,000 within the first year of publication, and 1943 before she reached 20,000 with *Five Little Pigs* (*Murder in Retrospect* in America)—perhaps a result of wartime dependence on the printed word for entertainment. Thereafter she never looked back and the Agatha Christie phenomenon becomes the Case of the Escalating Sales, with *Sparkling Cyanide*, called in America *Remembered Death* (1945), selling 30,000 within twelve months, and *The Hollow*, America's *Murder After Hours*, touching 40,000 in the following year. By 1950, when her fiftieth book, *A Murder Is Announced*, was published, the first printing was 50,000 and her subsequent crime books have never sunk below that figure. *Passenger to Frankfurt*, the 'extravaganza', as she called it, published to coincide with her eightieth birthday, beat all records, for by the end of the first year there were 58,000 copies in print. *Sleeping Murder*, the last Christie thriller of all and the final Miss Marple story, had a first printing of 60,000.

Despite the publicity attached to the recent star-studded film *Murder on the Orient Express*, Agatha Christie's success was never dependent on such outside stimulants. It is doubtful if the early plays and films based on her books significantly affected her sales. Until the outbreak of war in 1939 only two of her books had been dramatized—*Alibi* in 1928, from *The Murder of Roger Ackroyd*, and *Love from a Stranger* in 1936, based on the short story 'Philomel Cottage'; this was also filmed in 1937. But if stage and screen had less effect in the thirties than they do today, the coming of paperbacks intro-duced Agatha Christie to a new, avid and very faithful audience.

When Allen Lane founded Penguin Books in 1935, he was able to renew an old acquaintance, for he had handled Agatha Christie's early hardback books while working for his uncle John Lane at the Bodley Head. Now two of these early Christie titles, *The Mysterious Affair at Styles* and *Murder on the Links*, were among the fifteen original titles in the famous greenback crime series, Agatha Christie and Dorothy L. Sayers being the only two authors to be represented by two books each. In a surprisingly short time, Agatha Christie had become the first author after Bernard Shaw and H. G. Wells to have a million paperback copies of her books published on one day. Since then she has been published in Britain by Fontana, Pan and Penguin, and her books are reprinted constantly. In America, too, she has had several paperback publishers, among them Dell and Pocket Books.

By 1955 she had become a limited company, Agatha Christie Ltd. In 1968 the company was acquired by Booker Books, a subsidiary of Booker Brothers McConnell, who were anxious to diversify their traditional shipping, sugar-growing and rum-distilling interests. They had already acquired Ian Fleming, author of the James Bond books. Now, once again, they took a 51 per cent stake in the future work of a best-selling author—and they chose well. Even so, Agatha Christie remarked in 1970 that if she wrote more than one book a year she would only enlarge the finances of the Inland Revenue, 'who would spend it mostly on idiotic things'.

In 1965, inspired by the author's seventy-fifth birthday, Collins decided to bring out a collected edition of her works. The name Greenway Edition was chosen for the series, after Greenway House, Agatha Christie's Devonshire home. The first four titles were *The Labours of Hercules, Crooked House* (Agatha Christie's own favourite among her books), *A Murder Is Announced*, and of course *The Murder of Roger Ackroyd*.

Collins also published or republished a number of titles which do not fall within the Christie crime canon. These include *Star over Bethlehem* (1965), a collection of stories and poems for children, all with religious themes; a volume of autobiography, *Come, Tell Me How You Live*, originally published in 1946 and reprinted in 1975; six romantic novels under the name Mary Westmacott, originally published between 1930 and 1956 and republished in a uniform edition in 1973 and 1974; a play, *Akhnaton* (1973); and *Collected Poems* (1973), which contained her earlier volume of verse, *The Road of Dreams*, originally published in 1925 by Geoffrey Bles.

To a publisher's eye, she was one of the most professional of authors. Her typescripts arrived when she said they would. Her proofs were promptly corrected and returned. She did not care for any editing of her text, and as late as 1968 she wrote to Sir William Collins asking him to ensure that the spelling she used would not be changed unless a word had actually been misspelt; if there were two alternative spellings, she wanted her choice of spelling to be left alone. Similarly she objected to sentences being re-arranged to be more grammatically correct, especially in the case of spoken conversation, for this would make all the characters sound alike and not like ordinary variable human beings.

She liked to have a say in everything connected with her books, notably the jacket and the blurb. On one occasion, when by accident a jacket was not shown her, she wrote angrily protesting about this and saying that she wanted to see every jacket design before it was finalized because she hated having things put over on her. As this implies, she had strong views about jackets. She would never consent to any representation of Poirot, not even as played by Albert Finney in *Murder on the Orient Express;* and though she once allowed his patent-leather-shod feet to appear on the jacket of *Poirot's Early Cases*, she was never happy with even this partial representation. Her preference was always for a motif, and she herself drew the design for the three intertwined fish which appear on the jackets of the Greenway Edition.

She wrote fast and reckoned to complete a book in six weeks, working straight on to the typewriter and using three fingers instead of what she claimed was the more usual two, though her last few books were dictated straight on to the machine which Collins gave her for her eightieth birthday, because she had begun to find typing tiring. For a long time she averaged two books a year, and she maintained this output even during the war when circumstances such as paper shortage prevented such frequent publication. The result was two novels which she salted away, intending them to appear only after her death. In the case of *Curtain: Poirot's Last Case*, she was sufficiently impressed by the success of the film, *Murder on the Orient Express*, and the resulting interest in Poirot, to relent and allow it to be published in 1975.

Agatha Christie was a professional and she expected an equal degree of professionalism from her publishers. On one occasion—well remembered at Collins!—her author's copies of *Endless Night* failed to arrive before she left for a holiday in Spain. She wrote to say that she had been absolutely infuriated to see a whole array of *Endless Night* when she arrived at Heathrow airport and that, though she had found a parcel of books on her return home, these could hardly be called the author's 'advance copies'!

Besides a keen sense of what was properly due to an author, Agatha Christie was also very conscious of what was due to a work of creative imagination. She once replied to someone who wished to include an abridged passage from *The Body in the Library* in a modern language teaching series that, although it might be difficult for a person who was not himself an imaginative writer to appreciate, she felt making an abridged version of a creative author's book was like mutilating his brainchild. She said that she felt this to be true of any abridgement including recordings on tape. She did however allow her books to be serialized, and she was certainly aware of the difficulties of abridging, for she once tried to write a film version of her favourite Dickens novel, *Bleak House*—'such a good plot'—and discovered ruefully: 'The amount of characters in that book! I found I had to cut out many of the best ones.'

Although she was one of the world's biggest sellers, outsold only by the Bible and Shakespeare, Agatha Christie was remarkably modest. She never expected the day's work at Collins to be abandoned because she had crossed the threshold, and far from her craving publicity, her experience of it after the alleged 'disappearance' of 1926 caused her to shun it. She would never make a speech in public, not even at the party Collins gave to celebrate her eightieth birthday, when the leading literary editors came to do her homage.

But despite her reticence, she had the essential self-possession that comes from being born into a comfortable level of society—perhaps one might best describe it as the 'officer class', for her brother went into the army after leaving Harrow, and her first husband was a colonel in the Royal Flying Corps. It was evidently a station of life which suited her: an appropriate setting for the bridge and crossword puzzles and gardening which she so enjoyed. Her letters to her publishers give an occasional tantalizing glimpse of a comfortable way of life which, for all her vast earnings, never inclined to the ostentatious.

Nevertheless, within the limits of her secure and ordered world, Agatha Christie was always conscious of social change. 'When I re-read those first books,' she said in 1966, 'I'm amazed at the number of *servants* drifting about. And nobody is really doing any work, they're always having tea on the lawn.' In her fiftieth novel, *A Murder Is Announced*, she endeavoured to show some of the changes wrought in Miss Marple's village of St Mary Mead in the immediate post-war years. And the last book she wrote, *Postern of Fate*, published in 1974, contains a comment on one aspect of English life today which must have struck a responsive chord in many readers. 'He was used, now, to the general pattern of labour in the building trade, electrical trade, gas employees and others. They came, they showed efficiency, they made optimistic remarks, they went away to fetch something. They didn't come back. One rang up numbers on the telephone but they always seemed to be the wrong numbers. If they were the right numbers the right man was not working at this particular branch of the trade, whatever it was.'

Nor was her awareness of the need to move with the times confined to her books. In 1970 she wrote to her publisher saying that she had read a review of the Fontana series on Modern Masters. She asked if it would be possible to send her this series because she wanted to keep up to date and felt it would help her writing, and because she felt that Alexander *must* have an intelligent great-grandmother. The series includes such writers as Freud, Fanon, Chomsky and Wittgenstein. Alexander's great-grandmother was then eighty.

On 13 May 1976, exactly two weeks before the fiftieth anniversary of the first publication of *The Murder of Roger Ackroyd*, a memorial service for Agatha Christie was held at St Martin-in-the-Fields. At the request of her family, the address was given by Sir William Collins, her friend and publisher. It was the crowning tribute, on both sides, to a professional and personal relationship which had endured for half a century.

DOROTHY B. HUGHES

The Christie Nobody Knew

Everyone knew the Agatha Christie who created Hercule Poirot. She was the clever Christie, the one who thought up all manner of intricacies to tempt the attention of the reader and of the little Belgian detective. Almost as many knew the Mrs Christie who wrote of Miss Marple, illuminator of the English village, a lady in the complete sense of the word, genteel and imperturbable. In later years she would become a part of the Christie self-portrait. There were many who knew the Christie who, more or less as a pastime, wrote of that bright young couple, Tuppence and Tommy. And certainly, known to all her admirers was the Christie of centre stage, she who proved a writer could be at one and the same time equally successful as a playwright and as a novelist.

There was yet another Christie whom nobody knew, or so few as to amount to almost nobody. This was Mary Westmacott. Even today, and even in book circles, there are more who do not know than who do know her true identity.

Agatha Christie became Mary Westmacott in 1930 to write an unmystery novel, *Giant's Bread*. It caused rather less than a sensation. Four years later, Mary Westmacott tried again. Her second novel, *Unfinished Portrait*, like the first, made little to no imprint on the literary annals of the season.

From *Agatha Christie: First Lady of Crime*. © 1977 by Holt, Rinehart and Winston.

And so, Mary Westmacott disappeared. For ten years. Until 1944, when once again she entered the lists. It would seem her return was because she had a story that had to be told, a story which Agatha Christie could not tell. It was *Absent in the Spring*, and it is *la crème* of her small body of works. As before, all the beauty and emotion she poured into a work was as a libation wasted upon barren earth. She followed this one in 1947 with *The Rose and the Yew Tree*. It created no more stir than its predecessors.

Five years elapsed before she tried again. In 1952, *A Daughter's a Daughter* appeared, and in 1956 *The Burden*. They were received with the same lack of interest. With these she completed her six-novel offering. This was the end of Mary Westmacott's career.

Why? Why the waste of six unusual books, six fine books, six books which encompass some of the best of Christie's writing? There is no reason why anyone should pay a lick of attention to my answer to my question. True, it comes from a good many years of observation of the way of books. But it is no more than a personal opinion.

In my opinion then, Mary Westmacott's work was mishandled. Why else, before the secret was out, when it was no more than a murmur, was there always the addition of that disparaging throwaway line, 'not very good, woman-type stuff'. Woman-type indeed! As if Christie under whatever name would fashion a damozel shrinking through cold stony hallways and winding towers, her heart given to a dark and dour character whose bad manners and worse temper she mistakes for dislike, not affection, until the final passionate Gothic embrace. Or that Christie would have wasted her time telling of some silly modern girl who takes herself up into attics and down into cellars when she knows there is a killer loose and that she holds the clues to his or her identity.

The Westmacotts bear as little relation to women-type novels as to Winnie-the-Pooh. One cannot but wonder if any of those who proffered opinions had ever read her work. Had they, they would know that in its own way, each of these books, whose heroes lead lives of quiet desperation and whose villains are villainous only in that they do not understand, presents a fragment of the human comedy. Each tells a tale of the procession of days which add up to the years, and which resolve not in a crashing dissonance but in a whimper. And life goes on, but down a different lane and to a different bird call.

These are works in which Christie is trying to fathom herself and those who were a part of her world. The stories are the revelations of a woman of perception, a woman who is searching human emotions to preserve and heighten moments which must be remembered. She is writing of men and women whose dreams bleed when pricked, who are not beset by the gods or the fates, but who are made bereft by human frailties and a wanton expenditure of the loving heart.

Not by any catch-phrases can Westmacott be put into a Christie category. The books are not concerned with 'breathless romance, intrigue and suspense . . . tangled lives and star-crossed passions . . . dangerous secrets', as has been written of them. Westmacott was a distinctly different person from the mystery writer, Agatha Christie.

The six books are actually all a part of the same book. In the whole they are the fictionalized autobiography of Dame Agatha. Properly the autobiography begins with the second, *Unfinished Portrait* (1934). Christie could not have given many interviews before that time, at least not about her childhood and youth, or the Mary Westmacott identity would have been revealed immediately. In *Unfinished Portrait*, Larraby, a portrait painter, frames the story, thus making the pretence that it is a story, not a personal revelation. Yet there can be no doubt that Celia, the unknown woman he presumedly met and spoke with, is Christie, so much younger than others of her family that she is in effect an only child, the beloved of her mother.

Mary Westmacott writes beautifully of children: 'Then there were the things you thought about in the daytime. Nobody knew that as Celia walked sedately along the road she was in reality mounted upon a white palfrey. (Her ideas of a palfrey were rather dim. She imagined a super horse of the dimensions of an elephant.) When she walked along the narrow brick wall of the cucumber frames she was going along a precipice with a bottomless chasm at one side. She was on different occasions a duchess, a princess, a goose girl and a beggar maid. All this made life very interesting to Celia, and so she was what is called 'a good child', meaning she kept very quiet, was happy playing by herself, and did not importune her elders to amuse her . . . Celia seldom asked questions. Most of her world was inside her head. The outside world did not excite her curiosity.'

The book tells of her father's illness and early death, her mother travelling in grief, while the child lives with her superb grandmother:

> In figure she was majestically stout with a pronounced bosom and stately hips. She wore dresses of velvet or brocade, ample as to skirts, and well pulled in round the waist. 'I always had a beautiful figure, my dear,' she used to tell Celia. 'Fanny—that was my sister—had the prettiest face of the family, but she'd no figure—no figure at all! . . . As thin as two boards nailed together. No man looked at her for long when *I* was about. It's figure the men care for, not face.' 'The men' bulked largely in Grannie's conversation. She had been brought up in the days when men were considered to be the hub of the universe. Women merely existed to minister to these magnificent beings.

The character of Grannie in part prefigures Miss Marple.

> Grannie was never idle. She wrote letters—long letters in a
> spiky spidery handwriting, mostly on half sheets of paper,
> because it used them up, and she couldn't bear waste. ('Waste
> not, want not, Celia.') Then she crocheted shawls—pretty shawls
> in purples and blues and mauves. They were usually for the
> servants' relations. Then she knitted with great balls of soft fleecy
> wool. That was usually for somebody's baby. And there was
> netting—a delicate foam of netting round a little circle of
> damask. At tea time all the cakes and biscuits reposed on those
> foamy doilies . . .

And again:

> The night air, Grannie said, was highly injurious. Air of all
> kinds, indeed, she regarded as something of a risk. Except on the
> hottest days of summer she rarely went into the garden, such
> outings as she made were usually to the Army and Navy Stores—
> a four-wheeler to the station, train to Victoria, and another four-
> wheeler to the stores. On such occasions she was well wrapped
> up in her 'mantle' and further protected by a feather boa wound
> tightly many times round her neck.

It is this grandmother who takes the little girl on train trips to London,
where they lunch at the Army and Navy Stores, and Celia is introduced to
the magic of the theatre. All of Christie's girlhood is herein, the musical year
in Paris, the fashionable season in Cairo, the suitors and the proposals, the
love marriage which became the failed marriage, and which broke her beautiful world apart. In the end is the repetition of the beginning, as she, the
mother, is raising an only daughter. There is even included in this story her
own explanation of her strange disappearance and of an amnesia which was
less forgetting than dreaming. *Unfinished Portrait* is told with a minimum of
plot, in its stead is remembrance of times past. The portrait is unfinished as
her life was yet unfinished.

The first Westmacott, *Giant's Bread* (1930), was autobiographical only
in bits and pieces. It would seem to be the story of others she knew, knew
closely, composites to be sure because few if any writers go in for the verities
in their portraitures. Little Vernon has the same good no-nonsense nurse
that Celia will have, he even has the identical nursery wallpaper with 'mauve
irises twining upward'. Both children have dear imaginary playmates before

meeting with real children. Both are dreamers, of course, for the child Vernon, when not fictional is the child Celia.

> What was the word—the magic word? Brumagem—that was it—Brumagem. An enchanting word! The Princess Burmagem! A word to be repeated over to himself softly and secretly at night . . . Sitting on the slippery chintz, he frowned perplexedly. He had a sudden imperfect glimpse of two Mummies. One, the princess, the beautiful Mummy that he dreamed about, who was mixed up for him with sunsets and magic and killing dragons— and the other, the one who laughed and said, 'Aren't children too *funny*?' Only of course they were the same . . . He fidgeted and sighed.
>
> 'What's the matter, Master Vernon?'
>
> 'Nothing,' said Vernon. You must always say, 'Nothing.' You could never tell. Because if you did, no one ever knew what you meant . . .

Vernon, a girl cousin who comes to live with him and his mother, and a small London boy on the next estate, are inseparably tangled in each other's lives in maturity as well as in childhood.

In *Giant's Bread*, there is what must be mentioned, to us of the post-Hitlerian period, a familiar form of anti-Semitism. Yet Mary Westmacott, the product of her culture, her class, and her times, might well have considered her handling of Sebastian to be one of forthright liberalism. Vernon is an anti-hero, years before they became fashionable. Sebastian is the stable and sympathetic character, a Cambridge graduate, eventually an important London impresario, who is an intelligent businessman as well as a man of impeccable artistic taste. Westmacott's attitude to him must be little different from Queen Victoria's to Disraeli. He was a beloved friend, a man of fine character, brilliant in all respects, but always, the Jew.

In the ten-year period when Mary Westmacott lay fallow, Agatha Christie was, as we know, a whirlwind of activity, moving from honours and triumphs to the topmost Alp of the mystery field. Here she would remain. Yet Mary Westmacott could not be forgotten. She had more to say, and it could not be said in the medium in which Agatha Christie worked. The mystery novel, like the theatrical play or the sonnet, is contained within a prescribed pattern. The writer may wander a bit but not far, not and stay within the form.

When Mary Westmacott returned in 1944, she brought with her *Absent in the Spring*. Shakespeare gives the title and introduces the theme of the story, 'From you have I been absent in the Spring. . .' Of all the books created by either Christie or Westmacott, this one, even if it was born to blush almost unseen, must have given the most complete satisfaction, possibly even the exaltation which comes so rarely to a writer. For this is the perfect story, simple, bittersweet, ironic, expressing the heartbreak of love unfulfilled yet fulfilled.

The story concerns Joan, a wife and mother, who has never questioned her own values, who has managed a charming home for her husband and her three children, who has always done the proper thing. That her children married young to get away from home; that her husband, who wanted to farm the land, not become a solicitor, has retreated into himself, are facts which would never occur to her. Until she is marooned at a desert way-station *en route* from Baghdad, where she has been visiting her younger daughter, to Istanbul. She finishes reading her two books. She quickly uses up her bit of writing paper. And she is left with nothing, nothing but to learn about herself. Through her, Westmacott says that unless you have heights and depths, you are missing life, that there is a richness in the lives of those who know suffering, and an 'arid nothingness' in those who keep themselves insulated. In her blinding moments of self-revelation, Joan becomes aware of the love her husband had for another woman in their village, a woman who, to her, was nothing, nobody.

Little wonder the exquisite quality of this book was not discovered, when one reads that it concerns 'a husband's secret life' and 'the mysterious hold that beautiful Leslie Sherston had for him'. Compare Westmacott's design for Leslie Sherston: 'She walked through disillusionment and poverty and illness like a man walks through bogs and over plough and across rivers, cheerfully and impatiently, to get to wherever he is going. . .' The gallantry of Leslie and Rodney makes 'the unbearable bearable' as Archibald MacLeish said of poetry.

The theme of the desert, which is noted in one way or another in all the Westmacott books, is fully developed here. Westmacott distills the great clarity of desert light, the space and infinite solitude which compel a person to look into himself. And which also compel a person to know the presence of God. Perhaps the Westmacott readers alone are aware of what a strongly religious person Mrs Christie was. Prayer was a way of her life and the presence of God an integral part of living.

It is only meet that her next book should be inspired by both poetry and religion. The introduction and title of *The Rose and the Yew Tree* are from *Little Gidding*, the final section of T. S. Eliot's *Four Quartets*. 'The moment of the rose and the moment of the yew tree are of equal duration.'

The story is a retelling of the legend of Beauty and the Beast. But Westmacott does not accept its progress as simply a fairy tale. She asks:

Why? What impels Beauty to go by choice with the Beast? Why does she offer herself as sacrifice for him? The answer to all is love. Love which can be completed only in sacrifice. Yet this answer does not probe deeply enough for the author. Metaphysically she advances to the question: 'Does one ever really have a choice about anything?'

We do not know if Mary Westmacott became possessed by the riddle of time through her preoccupation with Eliot's poetry. Or if it was her dwelling upon the riddle which led her to Eliot. We do know that the theme of time is interwoven through all of the books, in the later ones in some depth. She ponders it in *The Rose and the Yew Tree*, but she does not evolve her final answer until *The Burden*, where, in the character of Mr Baldock, she states: 'The truth is, we're all slavishly obsessed by Time. Chronological sequence has no significance whatever. If you consider Eternity you can jump about in Time as you please. But no one does consider Eternity.'

It is no less in its people than in its themes that the books are all of a piece. Characters move from one setting to another, putting on a new name or face. Mr Baldock is part the nurse and part the grandmother, crusty but kind of heart. He is described as having a chair at the university, with a small cottage in the village where Laura, leading character of *The Burden*, when a little girl of ten, becomes his friend. On his first appearance he has invited Laura to tea but pretends he has forgotten the invitation. Later he tells her that he only made this pretence to see what she would say, and to have her see him as he is, 'a rude, ungracious old curmudgeon'. The tea he serves her is a child's dream tea, 'currant buns, jam roll, éclairs, cucumber sandwiches, chocolate biscuits and a large indigestible-looking rich black plum cake'. Laura gives 'a sudden little giggle', and confirms: 'You did expect me. Unless—do you have a tea like this every day?' 'God forbid,' said Mr Baldock. In another passage, his character is revealed in his reaction to a glimpse into Laura's dream world. '"Bad butter", said Mr Baldock. It was one of his expressions of perturbation. "Bad butter! Bad butter!"'

Mr Baldock is the only rock of Laura's world, both when she is a child and as an adult. As Nurse is Vernon's security, and, during her mother's illness, the grandmother is Celia's. Dame Laura in *A Daughter's a Daughter* may be a noted Harley Street practitioner, but in her more sophisticated habit she is the same commonsensical wise woman as Nurse and Nannie and Grandmother.

She is also in part another of the self-portraits of the later Christie: '"Like all old women, even if I am a distinguished one, I preach." She drains her glass of buttermilk and asks, "Do you know why I drink this?" "Because it's healthy?" "Bah! I like it. Always have since I went for holidays to a farm in the country. The other reason is so as to be different. One poses. We all pose. Have to. I do it more than most. But thank God, I know I'm doing it."'

It is through these character actors that Westmacott comes to terms with life. They are Chorus, wise, understanding, pragmatic.

The final two books, although entirely separate in the story sense, are at one in their theme. Sacrificial love destroys, not redeems. Oddly enough Westmacott uses the same name for a lead character in both. In the first, Dame Laura is the strength which manages, just, to save the mother and daughter from each other's devotion. In *The Burden*, Laura is the sister who takes on the burden of love. This is not the only instance where Westmacott repeats herself. Jim Grant, the freckle-faced boy farmer of *Unfinished Portrait*, becomes in *A Daughter's a Daughter* Jim Grant, army officer. One would consider it mere carelessness save that the books could not have been written carelessly, they are too finely wrought for that. It is true enough that most authors cannot remember character names from the opening to the closing of a book. Nevertheless with a favourite Christie character, which Dame Laura is, it is difficult to believe that in the very next book the name would be used again for a prominent character, not without purpose. Perhaps these oddities compose a cryptogram which we shall decipher when the yet unpublished Christie papers give us the proper clues.

For all the pain of living, these are not unhappy stories. There is in them affirmation of life, not its negation. Furthermore they give added values, such as we learned to expect from Christie in her sunset years. And there are moments of fun.

One of these extras comes in the closing book with Mary Westmacott's little lesson to readers. It may be a put-on, but it is more than that. Particularly for those who never learned to read Mary Westmacott properly. Mr Baldock asks the child Laura: 'How do you read a book? Begin at the beginning and go right through?'

When she replies, 'Don't you?' he tells her: 'No, I take a look at the start, get some idea of what it's all about, then go on to the end and see what the fellow has got to say and what he's been trying to prove. *Then* I go back and see how he's got there and what's made him land up where he did. Much more interesting.'

Laura says: 'I don't think that's the way the author meant his book to be read . . . I think you should read the book the way the author meant.' And the irrepressible Mr Baldock declaims: 'The reader's got rights too. The author writes the book the way he likes. Has it all his own way. Messes up the punctuation and fools around with the scene any way he pleases. And the reader reads the book the way *he* wants to read it, and the author can't stop him.'

AGATHA CHRISTIE

Growing Up

Life took on a completely different complexion after my father's death. I stepped out of my child's world, a world of security and thoughtlessness, to enter the fringes of the world of reality. I think there is no doubt that from the man of the family comes the stability of the home. We all laugh when the phrase comes, "Your father knows best," but that phrase does represent what was so marked a feature of late Victorian life. Father—the rock upon which the home is set. Father likes meals punctually; Father mustn't be worried after dinner; Father would like you to play duets with him. You accept it all unquestioningly. Father provides meals; Father sees that the house works to rule; Father provides music lessons.

Father took great pride and pleasure in Madge's company as she grew up. He enjoyed her wit and her attractiveness; they were excellent companions to each other. He found in her, I think, some of the gaiety and humour my mother probably lacked—but he had a very soft spot in his heart and affection for his little girl, the afterthought, little Agatha. We had our favourite rhyme:

> Agatha-Pagatha my black hen,
> She lays eggs for gentlemen,
> She laid six and she laid seven,
> And one day she laid eleven!

From *An Autobiography* by Agatha Christie. © 1977 by Dodd, Mead & Company.

Father and I were very fond of that particular joke.

But Monty, I think, was really his favourite. His love for his son was more than he would feel for any daughter. Monty was an affectionate boy, and he had great affection for his father. He was, alas, unsatisfactory from the point of view of making a success of life, and Father was unceasingly worried about this. In a way, I think, his happiest time, where Monty was concerned, was after the South African War. Monty obtained a commission in a regular regiment, the East Surreys, and went straight from South Africa, with his regiment, to India. He appeared to be doing well and to have settled down in his army life. In spite of father's financial worries, Monty at least was one problem removed for the time being.

Madge married James Watts about nine months after my father's death, though a little reluctant to leave Mother. My mother herself was urgent that the marriage should take place, and that they should not have to wait longer. She said, and truly I think, that it would be even more difficult for her to part with Madge as time went on and their companionship drew them closer. James's father was anxious for him to marry young. He was just leaving Oxford, and would go straight into the business, and he said it would be happier for him if he could marry Madge and settle down in their own home. Mr. Watts was going to build a house for his son on part of his land, and the young couple could settle down there. So things were arranged.

My father's American executor, Auguste Montant, came from New York and stayed with us a week. He was a large stout man, genial, very charming, and nobody could have been kinder to my mother. He told her frankly that father's affairs were in a bad mess, and that he had been extremely ill advised by lawyers and others who had pretended to act for him. A lot of good money had been thrown after bad by trying to improve the New York property by half-hearted measures. It was better, he said, that a good deal of the property should be abandoned altogether to save taxes. The income that was left would be very small. The big estate my grandfather had left had disappeared into thin air. H. B. Claflin & Co., the firm in which my grandfather had been partner, would still provide Grannie's income, as the widow of a partner, and also a certain income for Mother, though not a large one. We three children, under my grandfather's will, would get, in English currency, one hundred pounds a year each. The rest of the vast amount of dollars had been also in property, which had gone down the hill and fallen derelict, or had been sold off in the past for far too little.

The question arose now whether my mother could afford to live on at Ashfield. Here, I think, Mother's own judgment was better than anyone else's. She thought definitely that it would be a bad thing to stay on. The house would need repairs in the future, and it would be difficult to manage on a small income—possible but difficult. It would be better to sell the house and to buy another smaller house somewhere in Devonshire, perhaps near Exeter, which would cost less to run and would leave a certain amount of money from the exchange price to add to income. Although my mother had no business training or knowledge, she had really quite a lot of common sense.

Here, however, she came up against her children. Both Madge and I, and my brother, writing from India, protested violently against selling Ashfield, and begged her to keep it. We said it was our home and we couldn't bear to part with it. My sister's husband said he could always spare Mother a small addition to her income. If Madge and he came down in the summers they could help with the running expenses. Finally, touched I think by my violent love for Ashfield, Mother gave in. She said at any rate we would try how we got on.

I now suspect that Mother herself had never really cared for Torquay as a place to live. She had a great passion for cathedral towns, and she had always been fond of Exeter. She and my father sometimes went for a holiday touring various cathedral towns—to please her, I think, not my father—and I believe she rather enjoyed the idea of living in a much smaller house near Exeter. However, she was an unselfish person, and fond of the house itself, so Ashfield continued to be our home, and I continued to adore it.

To have kept it on was not a wise thing, I know that now. We could have sold it and bought a much more manageable house. But though my mother recognized that at the time, and must indeed have recognized it very much better later, yet I think she was content to have had it so. Because Ashfield has meant something to me for so many years. It has been there, my background, my shelter, the place where I truly belong. I have never suffered from the absence of roots. Though to hold on to it may have been foolish, it gave me something that I value, a treasure of remembrance. It has also given me a lot of trouble, worry, expense and difficulties—but surely for everything you love you have to pay some price.

My father died in November, my sister's marriage took place the following September. It was quiet, with no reception afterwards, owing to the mourning still observed for my father's death. It was a pretty wedding and took place in old Tor church. With the importance of being first brides-maid I enjoyed it all immensely. The bridesmaids all wore white, with white wreaths of flowers on their heads. The wedding took place at eleven in the morning, and we had the wedding breakfast at Ashfield. The happy couple were blessed not only with lots of lovely wedding presents but with every variety of torture that could have been thought up by my boy cousin Gerald and myself and the younger Wattses. All through their honeymoon rice fell out of every garment they removed from suitcases. Satin shoes were tied on to the carriage in which they drove away, and chalked on the back, after it had first been carefully examined to make sure that nothing of the kind had occurred, were the words "Mrs. Jimmy Watts is a first-class name." So off they drove to a honeymoon in Italy.

My mother retired to her bed exhausted and weeping, and Mr. and Mrs. Watts to their hotel—Mrs. Watts no doubt also to weep. Such appears to be the effect of weddings on mothers. The young Wattses, my cousin Gerald and I were left to view each other with the suspicion of strange dogs, and try to decide whether or not we were going to like each other. There was a great deal of natural antagonism at first between Nan Watts and me. Unfortunately, but in the fashion of the day, we had each been given harangues about the other by our respective families. Nan, who was a gay boisterous tomboy, had been told how nicely Agatha always behaved, "so quiet and polite." And while Nan had my decorum and general solemnity praised to her *I* had been admonished on the subject of Nan, who was said to be "never shy, always answered when she was spoken to—never flushed, or muttered, or sat silent." We both therefore looked at each other with a great deal of ill-will.

A sticky half-hour ensued, and then things livened up. In the end we organized a kind of steeplechase round the schoolroom, doing wild leaps from piled-up chairs and landing always on the large and somewhat elderly chesterfield. We were all laughing, shouting, screaming, and having a glorious time. Nan revised her opinion of me—here was somebody anything but quiet, shouting at the top of her voice. I revised my opinion of Nan as being stuck-up, talking too much, and "in" with the grown-ups. We had a splendid time, we all liked each other, and the springs of the sofa were permanently broken. Afterwards there was a snack meal and we went to the theatre, to *The Pirates of Penzance*. From that time the friendship never looked back, and continued intermittently all through our lives. We dropped it, picked it up, and things seemed just the same when we came together again. Nan went to live in Ireland, I lived in London. Later Nan lived in London too and we came together again. Then in the Second World War Nan sent her daughter to me in Devon for shelter, and arrived herself finally to take a house nearby in Devon. Nan is one of the friends I miss most now. With her, as with few others, we could talk together of Abney and Ashfield and the old days, the dogs, and the pranks we played, and our young men, and the theatricals we got up and acted in.

After Madge's departure the second stage of my life may be said to have begun. I was a child still, but the first phase of childhood had ended. The brilliance of joy, the despair of sorrow, the momentous importance of every day of one's life: these things are the hallmark of childhood. With them go security and the complete lack of thought for the morrow. We were no longer the Millers—a family. We were now just two people living together: a middle-aged woman, and an untried, naive girl. Things *seemed* the same, but the atmosphere was different.

My mother had had heart attacks since my father's death. They came on her with no warning, and nothing that the doctors gave her helped. I knew for the first time what it was to feel anxiety for other people, while at the same time being a child still, so that my anxiety was naturally exaggerated. I used to wake up at night, my heart beating, completely sure that mother was dead. Twelve or thirteen may be a natural time of anxiety. I knew, I think, that I was being foolish and giving way to exaggerated feelings, but there it was, I would get up, creep along the corridor, kneel down by my mother's door with my head to the hinge, trying to listen if I could hear her breathing. Very often I was quickly reassured—a welcome snore rewarded me! Mother had a special style of snoring, beginning daintily and pianissimo, and usually working up to a terrific explosion, after which she would usually turn over and there would be no repetition of the snoring for at least another three-quarters of an hour.

If I heard a snore then, delighted, I went back to bed and to sleep—but if there happened to be none, I remained there, crouching in miserable apprehension. It would have been far more sensible if I had opened the door and walked in to reassure myself, but somehow that does not seem to have occurred to me—or possibly Mother always locked her door at night. My grandmother always locked, bolted and barred herself in, and she probably had taught my mother, as a girl, to do the same thing. So long as my father was there, no question of locking the door would have arisen; protected by a strong man, a woman felt confident and assured.

I did not tell Mother about these terrible fits of anxiety, and I don't think she ever guessed at them. I used also to have fears, when she had gone out into the town, that she might have been run over. It all seems silly now, so unnecessary. It wore off gradually, I think, and probably lasted only for a year or two. Later I slept in Father's dressing room, off her bedroom, with the door slightly ajar, so that if she did have an attack in the night I could go in, raise her head, and fetch her brandy and sal volatile. Once I felt that I was on the spot, I no longer suffered from the awful pangs of anxiety—imagined fears diminished. I was, I suppose, always overburdened with imagination. That has served me well in my profession—it must, indeed, be the basis of the novelist's craft—but it can give you some very bad sessions in other respects.

The conditions of our life changed after my father's death. Social occasions practically ceased. My mother saw a few old friends but nobody else. We were very badly off and had to economize in every way. It was all we could do to keep up Ashfield. My mother no longer gave luncheon or dinner parties. She had two servants instead of three. She tried to tell Jane that we were now badly off and that she would have to manage with two young, inexpensive maids, but she stressed that Jane, with her magnificent cooking, could command a very large salary, and that she ought to have it. Mother would look about and find Jane a place where she would get good wages and also have a kitchen maid under her. "You deserve it," said my mother.

Jane displayed no emotion; she was eating at the time, as usual. She nodded her head slowly, continued to chew, then said: "Very well, ma'am. Just as you say—you know best."

The next morning, however, she reappeared—"I'd just like a word with you, ma'am. I've been thinking things over and I would prefer to stay here. I quite understand what you said, and I would be prepared to take less wages, but I have been here a very long time. In any case, my brother's been urging me to come and keep house for him and I have promised I will do so when he retires; that will probably be in four or five years' time. Until then I would like to stay here."

"That is very, very good of you," said my mother, emotionally. Jane, who had a horror of emotion, said, "It will be convenient," and moved majestically from the room.

There was only one drawback to this arrangement. Having cooked in one way for so many years, Jane could not stop cooking in the same strain. If we had a joint it was always an enormous roast. Colossal beefsteak pies, huge tarts and gargantuan steam puddings would be put on the table. Mother would say, "Only enough for two, remember, Jane," or "Only enough for four," but Jane could never understand. Jane's own scale of hospitality was terribly expensive for the household; every day of the week, seven or eight of her friends were wont to arrive for tea, and eat pastries, buns, scones, rock cakes and jam tarts. In the end, in desperation, seeing the household books mounting up, my mother said gently that perhaps, as things were different now, Jane would have one day a week when she could have her friends. This would save a certain amount of waste, in case a lot was cooked and then people did not turn up. Thenceforward Jane held court on Wednesdays only.

Our own meals were now very different from the normal three-or-four-course-feasts. Dinners were cut out altogether, and mother and I had a macaroni cheese or a rice pudding or something like that in the evening. I'm afraid this saddened Jane a great deal. Also, little by little, Mother managed to take over the ordering, which formerly had been done by Jane. It had been one of my father's friend's great delight, when staying in the house, to hear Jane ordering on the telephone in her deep bass Devonshire voice: "And I want six lobsters, *hen* lobsters, and prawns—not less than. . . ." It became a favourite phrase in our family. "Not less than" was not only used by Jane but also by a later cook of ours, Mrs. Potter. What splendid days for the tradesmen those were! My secretary once, living in the house when I was away, with her sister, complained, "It's all very well, you know, but I told Mrs. Potter we'd just like a few stewed figs for lunch—a quarter of a pound of dried figs would be quite enough. Instead of that, we had such an enormous dish of them that we had to eat stewed figs for a whole week!" Once a good cook gets certain quantities and sizes into her head it goes on like that.

"But I've always ordered twelve fillets of sole, ma'am," Jane would say looking distressed. The fact that there were not enough mouths to devour twelve fillets of sole, not even counting a couple in the kitchen, never appeared to enter her head.

None of these changes was particularly noticeable to me. Luxury or economy mean little when you are young. If you buy boiled sweets instead of chocolates the difference is not noticeable. Mackerel I had always preferred to sole, and a whiting with its tail in its mouth I always thought of as a most agreeable looking fish.

My personal life was not much altered. I read enormous quantities of books, and worked through all the rest of Henty and was introduced to Stanley Weyman (what glorious historical novels they were! I read *The Castle Inn* only the other day and thought how good it was).

The Prisoner of Zenda was my opening to romance, as it was for many others. I read it again and again. I fell deeply in love—not with Rudolf Rassendyll, as might have been expected, but with the real king imprisoned in his dungeon and sighing. I yearned to succour him, to rescue him to assure him that I—Flavia, of course—loved *him* and not Rudolf Rassendyll. I also read the whole of Jules Verne in French—*Le Voyage au Centre de la Terre* was my favourite for many months. I loved the contrast between the prudent nephew and the cocksure uncle. Any book I really liked I read over again at monthly intervals; then, after about a year, I would be fickle and choose another favourite.

There were also L. T. Meade's books for girls, which my mother disliked very much; she said the girls in them were vulgar and only thought of being rich and having smart clothes. Secretly, I rather liked them, but with a guilty feeling of being vulgar in my tastes! Some of the Hentys mother read aloud to me, though she was slightly exasperated by the length of the descriptions. She also read a book called *The Last Days of Bruce*, of which both she and I approved heartily. By way of lessons, I was put on to a book called

Great Events of History, of which I had to read one chapter and succeed in answering the questions about it set in a note at the end. This was a very good book. It taught a lot of main events that happened in Europe and elsewhere, which one could link on to the history of the Kings of England, from Little Arthur onwards. How satisfactory to be firmly told So-and-So was a bad king; it has a kind of Biblical finality. I knew the dates of the Kings of England, and the names of all their wives—information that has never been much use to me.

Every day I had to learn how to spell pages of words. I suppose the exercise did me some good, but I was still an extraordinarily bad speller and have remained so until the present day.

My principal pleasures were the musical and other activities into which I entered with a family called Huxley. Dr. Huxley had a vague but clever wife. There were five girls—Mildred, Sybil, Muriel, Phyllis and Enid. I came between Muriel and Phyllis, and Muriel became my special friend. She had a long face and dimples, which is unusual in a long face, pale golden hair, and she laughed a great deal. I joined them first in their weekly singing class. About ten girls took part in singing part-songs and oratorios under the direction of a singing master, Mr. Crow. There was also "the orchestra": Muriel and I both played mandolines, Sybil and a girl called Connie Stevens the violin, Mildred the 'cello.

Looking back on the days of the orchestra, I think the Huxleys were an enterprising family. The stuffier of the old inhabitants of Torquay looked slightly askance at "those Huxley girls," mainly because they were in the habit of walking up and down The Strand, which was the shopping center of the town, between twelve and one, first three girls, arm in arm, then two girls and the governess; they swung their arms, and walked up and down, and laughed and joked, and, cardinal sin against them, *they did not wear gloves.* These things were social offences at that time. However, since Dr. Huxley was by far the most fashionable doctor in Torquay, and Mrs. Huxley was what is known a "well connected," the girls were passed as socially acceptable.

It was a curious social pattern, looking back. It was snobbish, I suppose; on the other hand, a certain type of snobbishness was much looked down upon. People who introduced the aristocracy into their conversation too frequently were disapproved of and laughed at. Three phases have succeeded each other during the span of my life. In the first the questions would be: "But who *is* she, dear? Who are her *people?* Is she one of the *Yorkshire* Twiddledos? Of course, they are badly off, very badly off, but *she* was a *Wilmot.*" This was to be succeeded in due course by: "Oh yes, of course they *are* pretty dreadful, but then they are terribly *rich.*" "Have the people who have taken

The Larches got money?" "Oh well, then we'd better call." The third phase was different again: "Well, dear, but are they *amusing?*" "Yes, well of course they are not well off, and nobody knows where they came from, but they are very *very* amusing." After which digression into social values I had better return to the orchestra.

Did we make an awful noise, I wonder? Probably. The mandoline was at least painless. Anyway, it gave us a lot of fun and increased our musical knowledge. It led on to something more exciting, which was the getting up of a performance of Gilbert and Sullivan.

The Huxleys and their friends had already given *Patience*—that was before I joined their ranks. The next performance in view was *The Yeoman of the Guard*—a somewhat ambitious undertaking. In fact I am surprised that their parents did not discourage them. But Mrs. Huxley was a wonderful pattern of aloofness, for which, I must say, I admire her, since parents were not particularly aloof then. She encouraged her children to get up anything they liked, helped them if they asked for help and, if not, left them to it. *The Yeoman of the Guard* was duly cast. I had a fine strong soprano voice, about the only soprano they had, and I was naturally in the seventh heaven at being chosen to play Colonel Fairfax.

We had a little difficulty with my mother, who was old-fashioned in her views about what girls could or could not wear on their legs if they were to appear in public. Legs were legs, definitely indelicate. For me to display myself in trunk hose, or anything of *that* kind, would, my mother thought, be most indecorous. I suppose I was thirteen or fourteen by then, and already five foot seven. There was, alas, no sign of the full rich bosom that I had hoped for when I was at Cauterets. A Yeoman of the Guard's uniform was adjudged all right, though it had to be made with unusually baggy plus-four trousers!, but the Elizabethan gentleman presented more difficulties. It seems to me silly nowadays, but it was a serious problem then. Anyway, it was surmounted by my mother saying that it would be all right, but I must wear a disguising cloak thrown over one shoulder! So a cloak was managed out of a piece of turquoise blue velvet among Grannie's "pieces." (Grannie's pieces were kept in various trunks and drawers, and comprised all types of rich and beautiful fabrics, remnants which she had bought in various sales over the last twenty-five years and had now more or less forgotten about!) It is not terribly easy to act with a cloak—and it was draped over one shoulder and flung over the other, in such a way that the indelicacies of one's legs were more or less hidden from the audience.

As far as I remember I felt no stage fright. Strangely enough, for a terribly shy person, who very often can hardly bring herself to enter a shop, and who has to grit her teeth before arriving at a large party, there was one activity in which I never felt nervous at all, and that was singing. Later, when I studied both piano and singing in Paris, I lost my nerve completely whenever I had to play the piano in the school concert, but if I had to sing I felt no nervousness at all. Perhaps that was due to my early conditioning in "Is life a boon?" and the rest of Colonel Fairfax's repertoire. There is no doubt that *The Yeoman of the Guard* was one of the highlights of my existence. But I can't help thinking that it's as well that we didn't do any more operas—an experience that you really enjoyed should never be repeated.

One of the odd things in looking back is that, while you remember how things arrived or happened, you never knew how or why they disappeared or came to a stop. I cannot remember many scenes which I participated with the Huxleys after that time, yet I am sure there was no break in friendship. At one time we seemed to be meeting every day, and then I would find myself writing to Lully in Scotland. Perhaps Dr. Huxley left to practise elsewhere, or retired? I don't member any definite leave-taking. I remember that Lully's terms of friendship were clearly defined. "You can't be my *best* friend," she explained, "because there are the Scottish girls, the McCrackens. They have *always* been our best friends. Brenda is *my* best friend, and Janet is *Phyllis's* best friend; but you can be my second-best friend." So I was content with being Lully's second-best friend, and the arrangement worked well, since the "best friends," the McCrackens, were only seen by the Huxleys at intervals of, I should say, roughly two years.

II

It must, I think, have been some time in March that my mother remarked that Madge was going to have a baby. I stared at her. "Madge, have a *baby?*" I was dumbfounded. I cannot imagine why I shouldn't have thought of Madge having a baby—after all, it was happening all round one—but things are always surprising when they happen in one's own family. I had accepted my brother-in-law, James, or Jimmy, as I usually called him, enthusiastically, and was devoted to him. Now here was something entirely different.

As usual with me, it was some time before I could take it in. I probably sat with my mouth open for quite two minutes or more. Then I said "Oh—that *will* be exciting. When is it coming? Next week?"

"Not quite as soon as that," said my mother. She suggested a date in October.

"October?" I was deeply chagrined. Fancy having to wait all that time. I can't remember very clearly what my attitude to sex was then—I must have been between twelve and thirteen—but I don't think I any longer accepted the theories of doctors with black bags or heavenly visitants with wings. By then I had realized it was a physical process, but without feeling much curiosity or, indeed, interest. I had, however, done a little mild deduction. The baby was first *inside* you, and then in due course it was *outside* you; I reflected on the mechanism, and settled on the navel as a focal point. I couldn't see what that kind of round hole in the middle of my stomach was *for*—it didn't seem to be for anything else, so clearly it *must* be something to do with the production of a baby.

My sister told me years afterwards that she had had very definite ideas; that she had thought that her navel was a keyhole, that there was a key that fitted it, which was kept by your mother, who handed it over to your husband, who unlocked it on the wedding night. It all sounded so sensible that I don't wonder she stuck firmly to her theory.

I took the idea out into the garden and thought about it a good deal. Madge was going to have a baby. It was a wonderful concept, and the more I thought about it the more I was in favour of it. I was going to be an aunt— it sounded very grown-up and important. I would buy it toys, I would let it play with my dolls' house, I would have to be careful that Christopher, my kitten, didn't scratch it by mistake. After about a week I stopped thinking about it; it was absorbed into various daily happenings. It was a long time to wait until October.

Some time in August a telegram took my mother away from home. She said she had to go and stay with my sister in Cheshire. Auntie-Grannie was staying with us at the time. Mother's sudden departure did not surprise me much, and I didn't speculate about it, because whatever Mother did she always did suddenly, with no apparent forethought or preparation. I was, I remember, out in the garden on the tennis lawn, looking hopefully at the pear trees to see if I could find a pear which was ripe. It was here that Alice came out to fetch me. "It's nearly lunchtime and you are to come in, Miss Agatha. There is a piece of news waiting for you."

"Is there? What news?"

"You've got a little nephew," said Alice.

A nephew?

"But I wasn't going to have a nephew till October!" I objected.

"Ah, but things don't always go as you think they will," said Alice. "Come on in now."

I came in to the house and found Grannie in the kitchen with a telegram in her hand. I bombarded her with questions. What did the baby look like? Why had it come now instead of October? Grannie returned answers to these questions with the parrying art well known to Victorians. She had, I think, been in the middle of an obstetric conversation with Jane when I came in, because they lowered their voices and murmured something like: "The other doctor said, let the labour come on, but the specialist was quite firm." It all sounded mysterious and interesting. My mind was fixed entirely on my new nephew. When Grannie was carving the leg of mutton, I said:

"But what does he look like? What colour is his hair?"

"He's probably bald. They don't get hair at once."

"*Bald*, " I said, disappointed. "Will his face be very red?"

"Probably."

"How big is he?"

Grannie considered, stopped carving, and measured off a distance on the carving knife.

"Like that," she said. She spoke with the absolute certainty of one who knew. It seemed to me rather small. All the same the measurement made such an impression on me that I am sure if I were being asked an associative question by a psychiatrist and he gave me the key-word "baby" I would immediately respond with "carving knife." I wonder what kind of Freudian complex he would put that answer down to?

I was delighted with my nephew. Madge brought him to stay at Ashfield about a month later, and when he was two months old he was christened in old Tor church. Since his godmother, Norah Hewitt, could not be there, I was allowed to hold him and be proxy for her. I stood near the font, full of importance, while my sister hovered nervously at my elbow in case I should drop him. Mr. Jacob, our Vicar, with whom I was well acquainted, since he was preparing me for confirmation, had a splendid hand with infants at the font, tipping the water neatly back and off their foreheads, and adopting a slightly swaying motion that usually stopped the baby from howling. He was christened James Watts, like his father and grandfather. He would be known as Jack in the family. I could not help being in rather a hurry for him to get to an age when I could play with him, since his principal occupation at this moment seemed to be sleeping.

It was lovely to have Madge home for a long visit. I relied on her for telling me stories and providing a lot of entertainment in my life. It was Madge who told me my first Sherlock Holmes story, *The Blue Carbuncle*, and after that I had always been pestering her for more. *The Blue Carbuncle*, *The Red-Headed League* and *The Five Orange Pips* were definitely my favourites, though I enjoyed all of them. Madge was a splendid storyteller.

She had, before her marriage, begun writing stories herself. Many of her short stories were accepted for *Vanity Fair*. To have a Vain Tale in *Vanity Fair* was considered quite a literary achievement in those days, and Father was extremely proud of her. She wrote a series of stories all connected with sport—*The Sixth Ball of the Over*, *A Rub of the Green*, *Cassie Plays Croquet*, and others. They were amusing and witty. I reread them about twenty years ago, and I thought then how well she wrote. I wonder if she would have gone on writing if she had not married. I don't think she ever saw herself seriously as a writer, she would probably have preferred to be a painter. She was one of those people who can do almost anything they put their mind to. She did not, as far as I remember, write any more short stories after she married, but about ten or fifteen years later she began to write for the stage. *The Claimant* was produced by Basil Dean at the Royal Theatre with Leon Quartermayne and Fay Compton in it. She wrote one or two other plays, but they did not have London productions. She was also quite a good amateur actress herself, and acted with the Manchester Amateur Dramatic. There is no doubt that Madge was the talented member of our family.

I personally had no ambition. I knew that I was not very good at anything. Tennis and croquet I used to enjoy playing, but I never played them well. How much more interesting it would be if I could say that I always longed to be a writer, and was determined that some day I would succeed, but, honestly, such an idea never came into my head.

As it happened, I *did* appear in print at the age of eleven. It came about in this way. The trams came to Ealing—and local opinion immediately erupted into fury. A terrible thing to happen to Ealing; such a fine residential neighbourhood, such wide streets, such beautiful houses—to have *trams* clanging up and down! The word Progress was uttered but howled down. Everyone wrote to the press, to their M.P., to anyone they could think of to write to. Trams were common—they were noisy—everyone's health would suffer. There was an excellent service of brilliant red buses, with Ealing on them in large letters, which ran from Ealing Broadway to Shepherds Bush, and another extremely useful bus, though more humble in appearance, which ran from Hanwell to Acton. And there was the good old-fashioned Great Western Railway, to say nothing of the District Railway.

Trams were simply not needed. But they came. Inexorably they came, and there was weeping and gnashing of teeth—and Agatha had her first literary effort published, which was a poem I wrote on the first day of the running of the trams. There were four verses of it, and one of Grannie's old gentlemen, that gallant bodyguard of Generals, Lt.-Colonels, and Admirals, was persuaded by Grannie to visit the local newspaper office and suggest that it should be inserted. It was—and I can still remember the first verse:

> When first the electric trams did run
> In all their scarlet glory,
> 'Twas well, but ere the day was done,
> It was another story.

After which I went on to deride a "shoe that pinched." (There had been some electrical fault in a "shoe," or whatever it was, which conveyed the electricity to the trams, so that after running for a few hours they broke down.) I was elated at seeing myself in print, but I cannot say that it led me to contemplate a literary career.

In fact I only contemplated one thing—a happy marriage. About that I had complete self-assurance—as all my friends did. We were conscious of all the happiness that awaited us; we looked forward to love, to being looked after, to being cherished, and admired, and we intended to get our own way in the things which mattered to us while at the same time putting our husbands' life, career and success before all, as was our proud duty. We didn't need pep pills or sedatives, we had belief and joy in life. We had our own personal disappointments—moments of unhappiness—but on the whole life was *fun*. Perhaps it is fun for girls nowadays—but they certainly don't *look* as if it is. However—a timely thought—they may enjoy melancholy; some people do. They may enjoy the emotional crises that seem always to be over-whelming them. They may even enjoy anxiety. That is certainly what we have nowadays—anxiety. My contemporaries were frequently badly off and couldn't have a quarter of the things they wanted. Why then did we have so much enjoyment? Was it some kind of sap rising in us that has ceased to rise now? Have we cut it off with education and, worse, anxiety over education; anxiety as to what life holds for you?

We were like obstreperous flowers—often weeds maybe, but neverthe-less all of us growing exuberantly—pressing violently up through cracks in pavements and flagstones, and in the most inauspicious places, determined to have our fill of life and enjoy ourselves, bursting out into the sunlight, until someone came and trod on us. Even bruised for a time, we would soon lift a head again. Nowadays, alas, life seems to apply weed killer (selective!)—we have no chance to raise a head again. There are said to be those who are "unfit for living." No one would ever have told *us* we were unfit for living. If they had, we shouldn't have believed it. Only a murderer was unfit for living. Nowadays a murderer is the one person you *mustn't* say is unfit for living.

The real excitement of being a girl—of being, that is, a woman in embryo—was that life was such a wonderful gamble. *You didn't know what was going to happen to you.* That was what made being a woman so exciting. No worry about what you should be or do—Biology would decide. You were waiting for The Man, and when the man came, he would change your entire life. You can say what you like, that is an exciting point of view to hold at the threshold of life. What will happen? "Perhaps I shall marry someone in the Diplomatic Service . . . I think I should like that; to go abroad and see all sorts of places. . . ." Or: "I don't think I would like to marry a sailor; you would have to spend such a lot of time living in seaside lodgings." Or: "Perhaps I'll marry someone who builds bridges, or an explorer." The whole world was open to you—not open to your *choice*, but open to what Fate *brought* you. You might marry *anyone*; you might, of course, marry a drunkard or be very unhappy, but that only heightened the general feeling of excitement. And one wasn't marrying the profession, either; it was the *man*. In the words of old nurses, nannies, cooks and housemaids:

"One day Mr. Right will come along."

I remember when I was very small seeing one of mother's prettier friends being helped to dress for a dance by old Hannah, Grannie's cook. She was being laced into a tight corset. "Now then, Miss Phyllis," said Hannah, "brace your foot against the bed and lean back—I'm going to pull. Hold your breath."

"Oh, Hannah, I can't bear it, I can't really. I can't *breathe*."

"Now don't you fret, my pet, you can breathe all right. You won't be able to eat much supper, and that's a good thing, because young ladies shouldn't be seen eating a lot; it's not delicate. You've got to behave like a proper young lady. You're all right. I'll just get the tape measure. There you are—nineteen and a half. I *could* have got you to nineteen."

"Nineteen and a half will do quite well," gasped the sufferer.

"You'll be glad when you get there. Suppose this is the night that Mr. Right's coming along? You wouldn't like to be there with a thick waist, would you, and let him see you like that?"

Mr. Right. He was more elegantly referred to sometimes as "Your Fate."

"I don't know that I really want to go to this dance."

"Oh yes, you do, dear. Think! You might meet your Fate."

And of course that *is* what actually happens in life. Girls go to something they wanted to go to, or they didn't want to go to, it doesn't matter which—and there is their Fate.

Of course, there were always girls who declared they were not going to marry, usually for some noble reason. Possibly they wished to become nuns or to nurse lepers, to do something grand and important, above all self-sacrificial. I think it was almost a necessary phase. An ardent wish to become a nun seems to be far more constant in Protestant than in Catholic girls. In Catholic girls it is, no doubt, more vocational—it is recognized as one of the ways of life—whereas for a Protestant it has some aroma of religious mystery that makes it very desirable. A hospital nurse was also considered a heroic way of life, with all the prestige of Miss Nightingale behind it.

But marriage was the main theme; whom you were going to marry the big question in life.

By the time I was thirteen or fourteen I felt myself enormously advanced in age and experience. I no longer thought of myself as protected by another person, I had my own protective feelings. I felt responsible for my mother. I also began to try to know myself, the sort of person I was, what I could attempt successfully, and the things I was no good at and that I must not waste time over. I knew that I was not quick-witted, I must give myself time to look at a problem carefully before deciding how I would deal with it.

I began to appreciate time. There is nothing more wonderful to have in one's life than time. I don't believe people get enough of it nowadays. I was excessively fortunate in my childhood and youth, just *because* I had so much time. You wake up in the morning, and even before you are properly awake you are saying to yourself, "Now, what shall I do with today?" You have the choice, it is there, in front of you, and you can plan as you please. I don't mean that there were not a lot of things (duties, we called them) I had to do—of course there were. There were jobs to be done in the house: days when you cleaned silver photograph frames, days when you darned your stockings, days when you learned a chapter of *Great Events in History*, a day when you had to go down the town and pay all the tradesmen's bills. Letters and notes to write, scales and exercises, embroidery—but they were all things that lay in my choice, to arrange as I pleased. I could plan my day, I could say, "I think I'll leave my stockings until this afternoon; I will go down town in the morning and I will come back by the other road and see whether that tree has come into blossom yet."

Always when I woke up, I had the feeling which I am sure must be natural to all of us, a joy in being alive. I don't say you feel it consciously—you don't—but there you *are*, you are *alive*, and you open your eyes, and here is another day; another step, as it were, on your journey to an unknown place. That very exciting journey which is your life. Not that it is necessarily going to be exciting *as* a life, but it will be exciting to you because it is *your* life. That is one of the great secrets of existence, enjoying the gift of life that has been given to you.

Not every day is necessarily enjoyable. After that first delightful feeling of "Another day! How wonderful!" you remember you have to go to the dentist at 10:30, and that is not nearly so good. But the *first* waking feeling has been there, and that acts as a useful booster. Naturally, a lot depends on temperament. You are a happy person, or you are of a melancholic disposition. I don't know that you can do anything about *that*. I think it is the way one is made—you are either happy until something arises to make you unhappy, or else you are melancholy until something distracts you from it. Naturally happy people can be unhappy and melancholic people enjoy themselves. But if I were taking a gift to a child at a christening that is what I would choose: a naturally happy frame of mind.

There seems to me to be an odd assumption that there is something meritorious about working. Why? In early times man went out to hunt animals in order to feed himself and keep alive. Later, he toiled over crops, and sowed and ploughed for the same reason. Nowadays, he rises early, catches the 8:15, and sits in an office all day—still for the same reason. He does it to feed himself and have a roof over his head—and, if skilled and lucky, to go a bit further and have comfort and entertainment as well.

It's economic and necessary. But why is it *meritorious?* The old nursery adage used to be "Satan finds some mischief still for idle hands to do." Presumably little Georgie Stephenson was enjoying idleness when he observed his mother's tea-kettle lid rising and falling. Having nothing at the moment to do, he began to have ideas about it. . . .

I don't think necessity is the mother of invention—invention, in my opinion, arises directly from idleness, possibly also from laziness. *To save oneself trouble.* That is the big secret that has brought us down the ages hundreds of thousands of years, from chipping flints to switching on the washing-up machine.

The position of women, over the years, has definitely changed for the worse. We women have behaved like mugs. We have clamoured to be allowed to work as men work. Men, not being fools, have taken kindly to the idea. Why support a wife? What's wrong with a wife supporting *herself?* She *wants* to do it. By golly, she can go on doing it!

It seems sad that having established ourselves so cleverly as the "weaker sex," we should now be broadly on a par with the women of primitive tribes who toil in the fields all day, walk miles to gather camel-thorn for fuel, and on trek carry all the pots, pans and household equipment on their heads, while the gorgeous, ornamental male sweeps on ahead, unburdened save for one lethal weapon with which to defend his women.

You've got to hand it to Victorian women, they got their menfolk where they wanted them. They established their frailty, delicacy, sensibility—their constant need of being protected and cherished. Did they lead miserable, servile lives, downtrodden and oppressed? Such is not *my* recollection of them. All my grandmother's friends seem to me in retrospect singularly resilient and almost invariably successful in getting their own way. They were tough, self-willed, and remarkably well read and well informed.

Mind you, they admired their men enormously. They genuinely thought men were splendid fellows—dashing, inclined to be wicked, easily led astray. In daily life a woman got her own way while paying due lip service to male superiority, so that her husband should not lose face.

"Your father knows best, dear," was the public formula. The real approach came privately. "I'm sure you are *quite* right in what you said, John, but I wonder if you have considered. . . ."

In one respect man was paramount. He was the Head of the House. A woman, when she married, accepted as her destiny *his* place in the world and *his* way of life. That seems to me sound sense and the foundation of happiness. If you can't face your man's way of life, don't take that job—in other words, don't marry that man. Here, say, is wholesale draper; he is a Roman Catholic; he prefers to live in a suburb; he plays golf and he likes to go for holidays to the seaside. *That* is what you are marrying. Make up your mind to it and like it. It won't be so difficult.

It is astonishing how much you can enjoy almost everything. There are few things more desirable than to be an accepter and an enjoyer. You can like and enjoy almost any kind of food or way of life. You can enjoy country life, dogs, muddy walks, towns, noise, people, clatter. In the one there is repose, ease for nerves, time for reading, knitting, embroidery, and the pleasure of growing things; in the other theatres, art galleries, good concerts, and seeing friends you would otherwise seldom see. I am happy to say that I can enjoy almost everything.

Once when I was travelling by train to Syria, I was much entertained by a fellow traveller's dissertation on the stomach.

"My dear," she said, "never give in to your stomach. If a certain thing doesn't agree with you, say to yourself 'Who's going to be master, me or my stomach?'"

"But what do you actually do about it?" I asked with curiosity.

"Any stomach can be trained. Very small doses at first. It doesn't matter what it is. Eggs, now, used to make me sick, and toasted cheese gave me the most terrible pains. But just a spoonful or two of boiled egg two or three times a week, and then a little more scrambled egg and so on. And now I can eat any amount of eggs. It's been just the same with toasted cheese. Remember this, *your stomach's a good servant, but a bad master.*"

I was much impressed and promised to follow her advice, and I have done so—though it has not presented much difficulty, my stomach being definitely a servile one.

III

When my mother had gone abroad with Madge to the south of France after my father's death, I remained at Ashfield under the tranquil eye of Jane for three weeks by myself. It was then that I discovered a new sport and new friends.

Roller skating on the pier was a pastime much in vogue. The surface of the pier was extremely rough, and you fell down a good deal, but it was great fun. There was a kind of concert room at the end of the pier, not used in winter of course, and this was opened as a kind of indoor rink. It was also possible to skate at what was grandly called the Assembly Rooms, or the Bath Saloons, where the big dances took place. This was much more high class but most of us preferred the pier. You had your own skates and you paid twopence for admission, and once on the pier you skated! The Huxleys could not join me in this sport because they were engaged with their governess during the morning, and the same held for Audrey. The people I used to meet there were the Lucys. Although grown up, they had been very kind to me, knowing that I was alone at Ashfield because the doctor had ordered my mother abroad for change and rest.

Although I felt rather grand on my own, one could get weary of that feeling. I enjoyed ordering the meals—or thinking I was ordering the meals. Actually we always had for lunch exactly what Jane had made up her mind we were going to have beforehand, but she certainly put up a good show of considering my wildest suggestions. "Could we have roast duck and meringues?" I would ask, and Jane would say yes, but she was not sure about the ordering of the duck, and that perhaps meringues—there were no whites of egg at the moment, perhaps we had better wait until some day when we had used the yolks for something else; so that in the end we had what was already sitting in the larder. But dear Jane was very tactful. She always called me Miss Agatha and allowed me to feel that I was in an important position.

It was then that the Lucys suggested that I should come down and skate with them on the pier. They more or less taught me to stand up on my skates, and I loved it. They were, I think, one of the nicest families I have ever known. They came from Warwickshire, and the family's beautiful house, Charlecote, had belonged to Berkeley Lucy's uncle. He always thought that it ought to have come to him, but instead of that it had gone to his uncle's daughter, her husband taking the name of Fairfax-Lucy. I think the whole family felt very sad that Charlecote was not theirs, though they never said anything about it, except among themselves. The oldest daughter, Blanche, was an extraordinarily handsome girl—she was a little older than my sister and had been married before her. The eldest son, Reggie, was in the army but the second son was at home—about my brother's age—and the next two daughters, Marguerite and Muriel, known to all as Margie and Noonie, were also grown up. They had rather slurred lazy voices that I found very attractive. Time as such meant nothing to them.

After skating for some time, Noonie would look at her watch and say, "Well, did you ever, look at the time now. It's half-past one already."

"Oh dear," I said. "It will take me twenty minutes at least to walk home."

"Oh you'd better not go home, Aggie. You come home with us and have lunch. We can ring up Ashfield."

So I would go home with them, and we would arrive about half-past two to be greeted by Sam the dog—"Body like a barrel, breath like a drain-pipe," as Noonie used to describe him—and somewhere there would be some kind of meal being kept hot and we would have it. Then they would say it was a pity to go home yet, Aggie, and we would go into their schoolroom and play the piano and have a sing-song. Sometimes we went on expeditions to the moor. We would agree to meet at Torre station and take a certain train. The Lucys were always late, and we always missed the train. They missed trains, they missed trams, they missed everything, but nothing rattled them. "Oh well," they would say, "what does it matter? There'll be another one by and by. It's never any good *worrying*, is it?" It was a delightful atmosphere.

The high spots in my life were Madge's visits. She came down every August. Jimmy came with her for a few days, then he had to get back to business, but Madge stayed on till about the end of September, and Jack with her.

Jack, of course, was a never-ending source of enjoyment to me. He was a rosycheeked golden-haired little boy, looking good enough to eat, and indeed we sometimes called him "*le petit brioche*." He had a most uninhibited nature, and did not know what silence was. There was no question of bringing Jack out and making him talk—the difficulty was to hush him down. He had a fiery temper and used to do what we called "blow up"; he would first get very red in the face, then purple, then hold his breath, till you really thought he was going to burst, then the storm would happen!

He had a succession of nannies, all with their own peculiarities. There was one particularly cross one, I remember. She was old, with a great deal of untidy grey hair. She had much experience, and was about the only person who could really daunt Jack when he was on the warpath. One day he had been very obstreperous, shouting out "You idiot, you idiot, you idiot" for no reason whatever, rushing to each person in turn. Nannie finally reproved him, telling him that if he said it any more he would be punished. "I can tell you what I'm going to do," said Jack. "When I die I shall go to Heaven and I shall go straight up to God and I shall say 'You idiot, you idiot, you idiot.'" He paused, breathless, to see what this blasphemy would bring forth. Nannie put down her work, looked over her spectacles at him, and said without much interest:

"And do you suppose that the Almighty is going to take any notice of what a naughty little boy like you says?" Jack was completely deflated.

Nannie was succeeded by a young girl called Isabel. She for some reason was much addicted to throwing things out of the window. "Oh drat these scissors," she would suddenly murmur, and fling them out on to the grass. Jack, on occasions, attempted to help her. "Shall I throw it out of the window, Isabel?" he would ask, with great interest. Like all children, he adored my mother. He would come into her bed early in the morning and I would hear them through the wall of my room. Sometimes they were discussing life, and sometimes my mother would be telling him a story—a kind of serial went on, all about Mother's thumbs. One of them was called Betsy Jane and the other Sary Anne. One of them was good, the other was naughty, and the things they did and said kept Jack in a gurgle of laughter the whole time. He always tried to join in conversation. One day when the Vicar came to lunch there was a momentary pause. Jack suddenly piped up. "I know a very funny story about a bishop," he said. He was hastily hushed by his relations, who never knew *what* Jack might come out with that he had overheard.

Christmas we used to spend in Cheshire, going up to the Wattses. Jimmy usually got his yearly holiday about then, and he and Madge used to go to St. Moritz for three weeks. He was a very good skater, and so it was the kind of holiday he liked most. Mother and I used to go up to Cheadle, and since their newly built house, called Manor Lodge, was not ready yet, we spent Christmas at Abney Hall, with the old Wattses and their four children and Jack. It was a wonderful house to have Christmas in if you were a child. Not only was it enormous Victorian Gothic, with quantities of rooms, passages, unexpected steps, back staircases, front staircases, alcoves, niches— everything in the world that a child could want—but it also had three different pianos that you could play, as well as an organ. All it lacked was the light of day; it was remarkably dark, except for the big drawing room with its green satin walls and its big windows.

Nan Watts and I were fast friends by now. We were not only friends but drinking companions—we both liked the same drink, *cream*, ordinary plain, neat cream. Although I had consumed an enormous amount of Devon- shire cream since I lived in Devonshire, raw cream was really more of a treat. When Nan stayed with me at Torquay, we used to visit one of the dairies in the town, where we would have a glass of half-milk and half-cream. When I stayed with her at Abney we used to go down to the home farm and drink cream by the half-pint. We continued these drinking bouts all through our lives, and I still remember buying our cartons of cream in Sunningdale and coming up to the golf course and sitting outside the club house waiting for our respective husbands to finish their rounds of golf, each drinking our pinta cream.

Abney was a glutton's paradise. Mrs. Watts had what was called her storeroom off the hall. It was not like Grannie's storeroom, a kind of securely locked treasure house from which things were taken out. There was free access to it, and all round the walls were shelves covered with every kind of dainty. One side was entirely chocolates, boxes of them, all different, chocolate creams in labelled boxes. . . . There were biscuits, gingerbread, preserved fruits, jams and so on.

Christmas was the supreme Festival, something never to be forgotten. Christmas stockings in bed. Breakfast when everyone had a separate chair heaped with presents. Then a rush to church and back to continue present opening. At two o'clock Christmas dinner, the blinds drawn down and glittering ornaments and lights. First, oyster soup (not relished by me), turbot, then boiled turkey, roast turkey and a large roast sirloin of beef. This was followed by plum pudding, mince pies and a trifle full of sixpences, pigs, rings, bachelors' buttons and all the rest of it. After that, again, innumerable kinds of dessert. In a story I once wrote, *The Affair of the Christmas Pudding*, I have described just such a feast. It is one of those things that I am sure will never be seen again in this generation; indeed I doubt nowadays if anyone's digestion would stand it. However, *our* digestions stood it quite well then.

I usually had to vie in eating prowess with Humphrey Watts, the Watts son next to James in age. I suppose he must have been twenty-one or twenty-two to my twelve or thirteen. He was a very handsome young man, as well as being a good actor and a wonderful entertainer and teller of stories. Good as I always was at falling in love with people, I don't think I fell in love with him, though it is amazing to me that I should *not* have done so. I suppose I was still at the stage where my love affairs had to be romantically impossible—concerned with public characters, such as the Bishop of London and King Alfonso of Spain, and of course with various actors. I know I fell deeply in love with Henry Ainley when I saw him in *The Bondman*, and I must have been just getting ripe for the K.O.W.'s (Keen on Waller), who were all to a girl in love with Lewis Waller in *Monsieur Beaucaire*.

Humphrey and I ate solidly through the Christmas dinner. He scored over me in oyster soup, but otherwise we were neck and neck. We both first had roast turkey, then boiled turkey, and finally four or five slashing slices of sirloin of beef. It is possible that our elders confined themselves to only one kind of turkey for this course, but as far as I remember old Mr. Watts certainly had beef as well as turkey. We then ate plum pudding and mince pies and trifle. I rather sparingly of trifle, because I didn't like the taste of wine. After that there were the crackers, the grapes, the oranges, the Elvas plums, the Carlsbad plums and the preserved fruits. Finally, during the afternoon, various handfuls of chocolates were fetched from the storeroom to suit our taste. Do I remember being sick the next day? Having bilious attacks? No, never. The only bilious attacks I ever remember were those that seized me after eating unripe apples in September. I ate unripe apples practically every day, but occasionally I must have overdone it.

What I do remember was when I was about six or seven years old and had eaten mushrooms. I woke up with a pain about eleven o'clock in the evening, and came rushing down to the drawing room, where Mother and Father were entertaining a party of people, and announced dramatically: "I am going to die! I am poisoned by mushrooms!" Mother rapidly soothed me and administered a dose of ipecacuanha wine—always kept in the medicine cupboard in those days—and assured me that I was not due to die this time.

At any rate I never remember being ill at Christmas. Nan Watts was just the same as I was; she had a splendid stomach. In fact, really, when I remember those days, everyone seemed to have a pretty good stomach. I suppose people had gastric and duodenal ulcers and had to be careful, but I cannot remember anybody living on a diet of fish and milk. A coarse and gluttonous age? Yes, but one of great zest and enjoyment. Considering the amount that I ate in my youth (for I was always hungry) I cannot imagine how I managed to remain so thin—a scrawny chicken indeed.

After the pleasurable inertia of Christmas afternoon—pleasurable that is, for the elders: the younger ones read books, looked at their presents, ate more chocolates, and so on—there was a terrific tea, with a great iced Christmas cake as well as everything else, and finally a supper of cold turkey and hot mince pies. About nine o'clock there was the Christmas tree, with more presents hanging on it. A splendid day, and one to be remembered till next year, when Christmas came again.

I stayed at Abney with my mother at other times of year, and always loved it. There was a tunnel in the garden, underneath the drive, which I found useful in whatever historical romance or drama I was enacting at the moment. I would strut about, muttering to myself and gesticulating. I daresay the gardeners thought that I was mental, but I was on getting into the spirit of the part. It never occurred to me to write anything down—and I was quite indifferent to what any gardeners thought. I occasionally walk about nowadays muttering to myself—trying to get some chapter that won't "go" to come right.

My creative abilities were also engaged by embroidery of sofa cushions. Cushions were most prevalent at that time, and embroidered cushion covers always welcome. I went in for an enormous bout of embroidery in the autumn months. To begin with I used to buy transfers, iron them off on the squares of satin, and start embroidering them in silks. Disliking the transfers in the end as being all the same, I then began to take flower pictures off china. We had some big Berlin and Dresden vases with beautiful bunches of flowers on them, and I used to trace over these, draw them out, and then try to copy the colours as closely as possible. Granny B. was very pleased when she heard I was doing this; she had spent so much of her life in embroidery that she was glad to think a granddaughter took after her in that way. I did not reach her heights of fine embroidery, however; I never actually embroidered landscapes and figures, as she did. I have two of her fire screens now, one of a shepherdess, the other of a shepherd and shepherdess together under a tree, writing or drawing a heart on the bark of it, which is exquisitely done. How satisfying it must have been for the great ladies in the days of the Bayeux Tapestry, in the long winter months.

Mr. Watts, Jimmy's father, was a person who always made me feel unaccountably shy. He used to call me "dream-child," which made me wriggle in agonized embarrassment. "What is our dream-child thinking of?" he used to say. I would go purple in the face. He used to make me play and sing sentimental songs to him, too. I could read music quite well, so he would often take me to the piano and I would sing his favourite songs. I didn't like them much, but at least it was preferable to his conversation. He was an artistic man, and painted landscapes of moors and sunsets. He was also a great collector of furniture, particularly old oak. In addition he and his friend Fletcher Moss took good photographs, and published several books of photographs of famous houses. I wish I had not been so stupidly shy, but I was of course at the age when one is particularly self-conscious.

I much preferred Mrs. Watts, who was brisk, cheerful, and completely factual. Nan, who was two years older than I was, went in for being an enfant terrible, and took a special pleasure in shouting, being rude and using swear words. It upset Mrs. Watts when her daughter fired off *damns* and *blasts*. She also disliked it when Nan used to turn on her and say: "Oh don't be such a *fool*, Mother!" It was not the sort of thing that she had ever envisaged a daughter of hers saying to her, but the world was just entering into an age of plain speaking. Nan revelled in the role she was playing, though really, I believe she was quite fond of her mother. Ah well, most mothers have to go through a period in which their daughters put them through the mill in one way or another.

On Boxing Day we were always taken to the pantomime in Manchester—and very good pantomimes they were. We would come back in the train singing all the songs, the Wattses rendering the comedian's songs in broad Lancashire. I remember us all bawling out: "*I was born on a Friday, I was born on a Friday, I was born on a Friday when* (crescendo!) *my mother wasn't at 'ome!*" Also: "*Watching the trains coom in, watching the trains go out, when we'd watched all the trains coom in, we watched the trains go OUT.*" The supreme favourite was sung by Humphrey as a melancholy solo: "*The window, the window, I've pushed it through the window. I have no pain, dear Mother now, I've pushed it through the window.*"

The Manchester pantomime was not the earliest I was taken to. The first I ever saw was at Drury Lane, where I was taken by Grannie. Dan Leno was Mother Goose. I can still remember that pantomime. I dreamt of Dan Leno for weeks afterwards—I thought he was the most wonderful person I had ever seen. And there was an exciting incident that night. The two little Royal princes were up in the Royal Box. Prince Eddy, as one spoke of him colloquially, dropped his programme and opera glasses over the edge of the box. They fell in the stalls quite near where we were sitting, and, oh delight, not the Equerry but Prince Eddy himself came down to retrieve them, apologizing very politely, saying that he did hope they hadn't hurt anyone.

I went to sleep that night indulging in the fantasy that one day I would marry Prince Eddy. Possibly I could save his life from drowning first. . . . A grateful Queen would give her royal consent. Or perhaps there would be an accident—he would be bleeding to death, I would give a blood transfusion. I would be created a Countess—like the Countess Torby—and there would be a morganatic marriage. Even for six years old, however, such a fantasy was a little too fantastic to last.

My nephew Jack once arranged a very good royal alliance of his own at about the age of four. "Supposing, Mummy," he said, "you were to marry King Edward. I should become royalty." My sister said there was the Queen to be thought of, and a little matter of Jack's own father. Jack rearranged matters. "Supposing the Queen died, and supposing that Daddy"—he paused to put it tactfully—"supposing that Daddy—er— wasn't there, and then supposing that King Edward was to—just to *see* you. . . ." Here he stopped, leaving it to the imagination. Obviously King Edward was going to be struck all of a heap, and in next to no time Jack was going to be the King's stepson.

"I was looking in the prayerbook during the sermon," Jack said to me, about a year later. "I've been thinking of marrying you when I am grown up, Ange, but I've been looking in the prayerbook and there is a table of things in the middle, and I see that the Lord won't let me." He sighed. I told him that I was flattered that he should have thought of such a thing.

It is astonishing how you never really change in your predilections. My nephew Jack, from the days when he went out with a nursemaid, was always obsessed by things ecclesiastical. If he disappeared from sight you could usually find him in a church, gazing admiringly at the altar. If he was given coloured plasticine the things he made were always triptychs, crucifixes, or some kind of ecclesiastical adornment. Roman Catholic churches in particular fascinated him. His tastes never changed, and he read more ecclesiastical history than anyone I have ever known. When he was about thirty, he finally entered the Roman Catholic Church—a great blow to my brother-in-law, who was what I can only describe as the perfect example of a "Black Protestant." He would say, in his gentle voice:

"I'm not prejudiced, I really am *not* prejudiced. It's just that I can't help noticing that all Roman Catholics are the most terrible liars. It's not prejudice, it just *is* so."

Grannie was a good example of a Black Protestant too, and got much enjoyment out of the wickedness of the Papists. She would lower her voice and say: "All those beautiful girls disappearing into convents—*never seen again*." I am sure she was convinced that all priests selected their mistresses from special convents of beautiful girls.

The Watts were nonconformists, Methodist I think, which perhaps may have led to this tendency to regard Roman Catholics as representatives of "the Scarlet Woman of Babylon." Where Jack got his passion for the Roman Catholic Church I cannot think. He doesn't seem to have inherited it from anyone in his family, but it was there, present always from his early years. Everybody took a great interest in religion in my young days. Disputes about it were full and colourful, and sometimes heated. One of my nephew's friends said to him later in life: "I really can't think, Jack, why you can't be a cheerful heretic like everyone else, it would be so much more peaceful."

The last thing on earth that Jack could ever imagine being was peaceful. As his nursemaid said, on one occasion, when she had spent some time finding him, "Why Master Jack wants to go into churches, I can't imagine. It seems such a funny thing for a child to want to do." Personally, I think he must have been a reincarnation of a medieval churchman. He had, as he grew older, what I might call a churchman's face—not a monk's face, certainly not a visionary's—the kind of churchman versed in ecclesiastical practices and able to acquit himself well at the Council of Trent—and to be quite sound on the exact number of angels able to dance on the point of a needle.

IV

Bathing was one of the joys of my life, and has remained so almost until my present age; in fact I would still enjoy it as much as ever but for the difficulties attendant on a rheumatic person getting herself into the water, and, even more difficult, out again.

A great social change came when I was about thirteen. Bathing as I first remember it was strictly segregated. There was a special Ladies'

Bathing Cove, a small stony beach, to the left of the Bath Saloons. The beach was a steeply sloping one, and on it there were eight bathing machines in the charge of an ancient man, of somewhat irascible temper, whose nonstop job was to let the machines up and down in the water. You entered your bathing machine—a gaily painted striped affair—saw that both doors were safely bolted, and began to undress with a certain amount of caution, because at any moment the elderly man might decide it was your turn to be let down into the water. At that moment there would be a frantic rocking, and the bathing machine would grind its way slowly over the loose stones, flinging you about from side to side. In fact the action was remarkably similar to that of a Jeep or Land Rover nowadays, when traversing the more rocky parts of the desert.

The bathing machine would stop as suddenly as it had started. You then proceeded with your undressing and got into your bathing dress. This was an unaesthetic garment, usually made of dark blue or black alpaca, with numerous skirts, flounces and frills, reaching well down below the knees, and over the elbow. Once fully attired, you unbolted the door on the water side. If the old man had been kind to you, the top step was practically level with the water. You descended and there you were, decorously up to your waist. You then proceeded to swim. There was a raft not too far out, to which you could swim and pull yourself up and sit on it. At low tide it was quite near; at high tide it was quite a good swim, and you had it more or less to yourself. Having bathed as long as you liked, which for my part was a good deal longer than any grownup accompanying me was inclined to sanction, you were signalled to come back to shore—but as they had difficulty in getting at me once I was safely on the raft, and anyway I proceeded to swim in the opposite direction, I usually managed to prolong it to my own pleasure.

There was of course no such thing as sunbathing on the beach. Once you left the water you got into your bathing machine, you were drawn up with the same suddenness with which you had been let down, and finally emerged, blue in the face, shivering all over, with hands and cheeks died away to a state of numbness. This, I may say, never did me any harm, and I was as warm as toast again in about three-quarters of an hour. I then sat on the beach and ate a bun while I listened to exhortations on my bad conduct in not having come out sooner. Grannie, who always had a fine series of cautionary tales, would explain to me how Mrs. Fox's little boy ("such a lovely creature") had gone to his death of pneumonia, entirely from disobeying his elders and staying in the sea too long. Partaking of my currant bun, or whatever refreshment I was having, I would reply dutifully, "No, Grannie, I won't stay in as long next time. But actually, Grannie, the water was really *warm*."

"Really warm, was it indeed? Then why are you shivering from head to foot? Why are your fingers so blue?"

The advantage of being accompanied by a grown-up person, especially Grannie, was that we would go home in a cab from the Strand, instead of having to walk a mile and a half. The Torbay Yacht Club was stationed on Beacon Terrace, just above the Ladies' Bathing Cove, and although the beach was properly invisible from the club windows, the sea around the raft was not, and, according to my father, a good many of the gentlemen spent their time with opera glasses enjoying the sight of female figures displayed in what they hopefully thought of as almost a state of nudity! I don't think we can have been sexually very appealing in those shapeless garments.

The Gentlemen's Bathing Cove was situated farther along the coast. There the gentlemen, in their scanty triangles, could disport themselves as much as they pleased, with no female eye able to observe them from any point whatever. However, times were changing: mixed bathing was being introduced all over England.

The first thing mixed bathing entailed was wearing far more clothing than before. Even French ladies had always bathed in stockings, so that no sinful bare legs could be observed. I have no doubt that, with natural French chic, they managed to cover themselves from their necks to their wrists, and with lovely thin silk stockings outlining their beautiful legs, looked far more sinfully alluring than if they had worn a good old short-skirted British bathing dress of frilled alpaca. I really don't know why legs were considered so improper: throughout Dickens there are screams when any lady thinks that her ankles have been observed. The very word was considered daring. One of the first nursery axioms was always uttered if you mentioned those pieces of your anatomy: "Remember, the Queen of Spain has no legs." "What does she have instead, Nursie?" "*Limbs*, dear, that is what we call them; arms and legs are limbs."

All the same, I think it would sound odd to say: "I've got a spot coming on one of my limbs, just below the knee."

Which reminds me of a friend of my nephew's, who described an experience of her own as a little girl. She had been told that her godfather was coming to see her. Having not heard of such a personage before, she had been thrilled by the notion. That night, at about one A.M., after waking and considering the matter for some time, she spoke into the darkness:

"Nanny, I've got a godfather."

"Urmrp." Some indescribable sound answered her.

"Nanny," a little louder, "I've got a *godfather*."

"Yes, dear, yes, very nice."

"But, Nanny, I've got a—fortissimo—"GODFATHER.""

"Yes, yes, turn over, dear, and go to sleep."

"But, Nanny"—molto fortissimo—"I HAVE GOT A GODFATHER!"

"Well, *rub* it, dearie, *rub* it!"

Bathing dresses continued to be very pure practically up to the time I was first married. Though mixed bathing was accepted by then, it was still regarded as dubious by the older ladies and more conservative families. But progress was too strong, even for my mother. We often took to the sea on such beaches as were given over to the mingling of the sexes. It was allowed first on Tor Abbey Sands and Corbin's Head Beach, which were more or less main town beaches. We did not bathe there anyway—our beaches were supposed to be too crowded. Then mixed bathing was allowed on the more aristocratic Meadfoot Beach. This was another good twenty minutes away, and therefore made your walk to bathe rather a long one, practically two miles. However, Meadfoot Beach was much more attractive than the Ladies' Bathing Cove: bigger, wider, with an accessible rock a good way out to which you could swim if you were a strong swimmer. The Ladies' Bathing Cove remained sacred to segregation, and the men were left in peace in their dashing triangles. As far as I remember, the men were not particularly anxious to avail themselves of the joys of mixed bathing; they stuck rigidly to their own private preserve. Such of them as arrived at Meadfoot were usually embarrassed by the sight of their sisters' friends in what they still considered a state of near nudity.

It was at first the rule that I should wear stockings when I bathed. I don't know how French girls kept their stockings on: I was quite unable to do so. Three or four vigorous kicks when swimming, and my stockings were dangling a long way beyond my toes; they were either sucked off altogether or else wrapped round my ankles like fetters by the time I emerged. I think that the French girls one saw bathing in fashion plates owed their smartness to the fact that they never actually swam, only walked gently into the sea and out again, to parade the beach.

A pathetic tale was told of the Council Meeting at which the question of mixed bathing came up for final approval. A very old Councillor, a vehement opponent, finally defeated, quavered out his last plea:

"And all I say is, Mr. Mayor, if this 'ere mixed bathing is carried through, that there will be decent partitions in the bathing machines, *however low*."

With Madge bringing down Jack every summer to Torquay, we bathed practically every day. Even if it rained or blew a gale, it seems to me that we still bathed. In fact, on a rough day I enjoyed the sea even more.

Very soon there came the great innovation of trams. One could catch a tram at the bottom of Burton Road and be taken down to the harbour, and from there it was only about twenty minutes' walk to Meadfoot. When Jack was about five, he started to complain. "What about taking a cab from the tram to the beach?" "Certainly not," said my sister, horrified. "We've come down all this way in a tram, haven't we? Now we walk to the beach."

My nephew would sigh and say under his breath, "Mum on the stingy side again."

In retaliation, as we walked up the hill, which was bordered on either side with Italianate villas, my nephew, who, at that age, never stopped talking for a moment, would proceed with a kind of Gregorian chant of his own, which consisted of repeating the names of all the houses we passed: "Lanka, Pentreave, The Elms, Villa Marguerita, Hartly St. George." As time went on, he added the names of such occupants as he knew, starting with "Lanka, Dr. G. Wreford; Pentreave, Dr. Quick; Villa Marguerita, Madam Cavallen; The Laurels, don't know," and so on. Finally, infuriated, Madge or I would tell him to shut up".

"Why?"

"Because we want to talk to each other, and we can't talk to each other if you are talking the whole time and interrupting us."

"Oh, very well." Jack lapsed into silence. His lips were moving, however, and one could just hear in faint breath: "Lanka, Pentreave, The Priory, Torbay Hall. . . ." Madge and I would look at each other and try to think of something to say.

Jack and I nearly drowned ourselves one summer. It was a rough day; we had not gone as far as Meadfoot, but instead to the Ladies' Bathing Cove, where Jack was not yet old enough to cause a tremor in female breasts. He could not swim at that time, or only a few strokes, so I was in the habit of taking him out to the raft on my back. On this particular morning we started off as usual, but it was a curious kind of sea—a sort of mixed swell and chop—and, with the additional weight on my shoulders, I found it almost impossible to keep my mouth and nose above water. I was swimming, but I couldn't get any breath into myself. The tide was not far out, so that the raft was quite close, but I was making little progress, and was only able to get a breath about every third stroke.

Suddenly I realized that I could not make it. At any moment now I was going to choke. "Jack," I gasped, "get off and swim to the raft. You're nearer that than the shore." "Why?" said Jack, "I don't want to." "Please—do—" I bubbled. My head went under. Fortunately, though Jack clung to me at first, he got shaken off and was able therefore to proceed under his own steam. We were quite near the raft by then, and he reached it with no difficulty. By that time I was past noticing what anyone was doing. The only feeling in my mind was a great sense of indignation. I had always been told that when you were drowning the whole of your past life came before you, and I had also been told that you heard beautiful music when you were dying. There was no beautiful music, and I couldn't think about anything in my past life; in fact I could think of nothing at all but how I was going to get some breath into my lungs. Everything went black and—and—and the next thing I knew was violent bruises and pains as I was flung roughly into a boat. The old Sea-Horse, crotchety and useless as we had always thought him, had had enough sense to notice that somebody was drowning and had come out in the boat allowed him for the purpose. Having thrown me into the boat he took a few more strokes to the raft and grabbed Jack, who resisted loudly saying, "I don't want to go in yet. I've only just got here, I want to play on the raft. I won't come in! The assorted boatload reached the shore, and my sister came down the beach laughing heartily and saying, "What were you doing? What's all this fuss?"

"Your sister nearly drowned herself," said the old man crossly. "Go on, take this child of yours. We'll lay her out flat, and we'll see if she needs a bit of punching."

I suppose they gave me a bit of punching, though I don't think I had quite lost consciousness.

"I can't see how you knew she was drowning. Why didn't she shout for help?"

"I keeps an eye. Once you goes down you can't shout—water's comin' in."

We both thought highly of the old Sea-Horse after that.

The outside world impinged much less than it had in my father's time. I had my friends and my mother had one or two close friends whom she saw, but there was little social interchange. For one thing Mother was very badly off; she had no money to spare for social entertainments, or indeed for paying cab fares to go to luncheons or dinners. She had never been a great walker, and now, with her heart attacks, she got out little, as it was impossible in Torquay to go anywhere without going up or down hill almost immediately. I had bathing in the summer, roller skating in the winter and masses of books to read. There, of course, I was constantly making new discoveries. Mother read me Dickens aloud at this point and we both enjoyed it.

Reading aloud started with Sir Walter Scott. One of my favourites was *The Talisman*. I also read *Marmion* and *The Lady of the Lake*, but I think that both Mother and I were highly pleased when we passed from Sir Walter Scott to Dickens. Mother, impatient as always, did not hesitate to skip when it suited her fancy. "All these descriptions," she would say at various points in Sir Walter Scott. "Of course they are very good, and literary, but one can have too many of them." I think she also cheated by missing out a certain amount of sob stuff in Dickens, particularly the bits about Little Nell.

Our first Dickens was *Nicholas Nickleby*, and my favourite character was the old gentleman who courted Mrs. Nickleby by throwing vegetable marrows over the wall. Can this be one of the reasons why I made Hercule Poirot retire to grow vegetable marrows? Who can say? My favourite Dickens of all was *Bleak House*, and still is.

Occasionally we would try Thackeray for a change. We got through *Vanity Fair* all right, but we stuck on *The Newcombes*—"We ought to like it," said my mother, "everyone says it is his best." My sister's favourite had been *Esmond*, but that too we found diffuse and difficult; indeed I have never been able to appreciate Thackeray as I should.

For my own reading, the works of Alexandre Dumas in French now entranced me. *The Three Musketeers, Twenty Years After* and, best of all, *The Count of Monte Cristo*. My favourite was the first volume, *Le Château d'If*, but although the other five volumes occasionally had me slightly bewildered, the whole colourful pageant of the story was entrancing. I also had a romantic attachment to Maurice Howlett: *The Forest Lovers, The Queen's Quair* and *Richard Yea-and-Nay*. Very good historical novels they are, too.

Occasionally my mother would have a sudden idea. I remember one day when I was picking up suitable windfalls from the apple tree, she arrived like a whirlwind from the house. "Quickly," she said. "We are going to Exeter."

"Going to Exeter," I said surprised. "Why?"

"Because Sir Henry Irving is playing there, in *Becket*. He may not live much longer, and you *must* see him. A great actor. We've just time to catch the train. I have booked a room at the hotel."

We duly went to Exeter, and it was indeed a wonderful performance of *Becket* which I have never forgotten.

The theatre had never stopped being a regular part of my life. When staying at Ealing, Grannie used to take me to the theatre at least once a week, sometimes twice. We went to all the musical comedies, and she used to buy me the score afterwards. Those scores—how I enjoyed playing them! At Ealing, the piano was in the drawing room, and so fortunately I did not annoy anyone by playing several hours on end.

The drawing room at Ealing was a wonderful period piece. There was practically no room in it to move about. It had a rather splendid thick Turkey carpet on the floor, and every type of brocaded chair; each one of them uncomfortable. It had two, if not three, marquetry china cabinets, a large central candelabra, standard oil lamps, quantities of small whatnots, occasional tables, and French Empire furniture. The light from the window was blocked by a conservatory, a prestige symbol that was a must, as in all self-respecting Victorian houses. It was a very cold room; the fire was only lit there if we had a party; and nobody as a rule went into it except myself. I would light the brackets on the piano, adjust the music stool, breathe heavily on my fingers, and start off with *The Country Girl* or *Our Miss Gibbs*. Sometimes I allotted roles to "the girls," sometimes I was myself singing them, a new and unknown star.

Taking my scores to Ashfield, I used to play them in the evenings in the schoolroom (also an icy cold room in winter). I played and I sang. Mother often used to go to bed early, after a light supper, about eight o'clock. After she had had about two and a half hours of me thumping a piano overhead, and singing at the top of my voice, she could bear it no longer, and used to take a long pole, which was used for pushing the windows up and down, and rap frantically on the ceiling with it. Regretfully I would abandon my piano.

I also invented an operetta of my own called *Marjorie*. I did not compose it exactly, but I sang snatches of it experimentally in the garden. I had some vague idea that I might really be able to write and compose music one day. I got as far as the libretto, and there I stuck. I can't remember the whole story now but it was all slightly tragic, I think. A handsome young man with a glorious tenor voice loved desperately a girl called Marjorie, who equally naturally did not love him in return. In the end he married another girl, but on the day after his wedding a letter arrived from Marjorie in a far country saying that she was dying and had at last realized that she loved him. He left his bride and rushed to her forthwith. She was not quite dead when he arrived—alive enough at any rate to raise herself on one elbow and sing a splendid dying love song. The bride's father arrived to wreak vengeance for his deserted daughter, but was so affected by the lovers' grief that he joined his baritone to their voices and one of the most famous trios ever written concluded the opera.

I also had a feeling that I might like to write a novel called *Agnes*. I remember even less of that. It had four sisters in it: Queenie, the eldest, golden-haired and beautiful, and then some twins, dark and handsome, finally Agnes, who was plain, shy and (of course) in poor health, lying patiently on a sofa. There must have been more story than this, but it has all gone now. All I can remember is that Agnes's true worth was recognized at last by some splendid man with a black moustache whom she had loved secretly for many years.

The next of my mother's sudden ideas was that perhaps, after all, I wasn't being educated enough, and that I had better have a little schooling. There was a girls' school in Torquay kept by someone called Miss Guyer, and my mother made an arrangement that I should go there two days a week and study certain subjects. I think one was arithmetic, and there was also grammar and composition. I enjoyed arithmetic, as always, and may even have begun algebra there.

Grammar I could not understand in the least: I could not see *why* certain things were called prepositions or what verbs were supposed to *do*, and the whole thing was a foreign language to me. I used to plunge happily into composition, but not with real success. The criticism was always the same: my compositions were too fanciful. I was severely criticized for not keeping to the subject. I remember—"Autumn"—in particular. I started off well, with golden and brown leaves, but suddenly, somehow or other, a *pig* got into it—I think it was possibly rooting up acorns in the forest. Anyway, I got interested in the pig, forgot all about autumn, and the composition ended with the riotous adventures of Curlytail the Pig and a terrific Beechnut Party he gave his friends.

I remember one teacher there—I can't recall her name now. She was short and spare, and I remember her eager jutting chin. Quite unexpectedly one day (in the middle, I think, of an arithmetic lesson) she suddenly launched forth on a speech on life and religion. "All of you," she said, "every *one* of you—will pass through a time when you will face despair. If you never face despair, you will never have faced, or become, a Christian, or known a Christian life. To be a Christian you must face and accept the life that Christ faced and lived; you must enjoy things as he enjoyed things; be as happy as he was at the marriage at Canaan, know the peace and happiness that it means to be in harmony with God and with God's will. But you must also know, as he did, what it means to be alone in the Garden of Gethsemane, to feel that all your friends have forsaken you, that those you love and trust have turned away from you, and that *God Himself* has forsaken you. Hold on then to the belief that that is *not* the end. If you love, you will suffer, and if you do not love, you do not know the meaning of a Christian life."

She then returned to the problems of compound interest with her usual vigour, but it is odd that those few words, more than any sermon I have ever heard, remained with me, and years later they were to come back to me and give me hope at a time when despair had me in its grip. She was a dynamic figure, and also, I think, a *fine* teacher; I wish I could have been taught by her longer.

Sometimes I wonder what would have happened if I had continued with my education. I should, I suppose, have progressed, and I think I should have been entirely caught up in mathematics—a subject which has always fascinated me. If so, my life would certainly have been very different. I should have been a third- or fourth-rate mathematician and gone through life quite happily. I should probably not have written any books. Mathematics and music would have been enough to satisfy me. They would have engaged my attention, and shut out the world of imagination.

On reflection, though, I think that you are what you are going to be. You indulge in the fantasies of, "If so-and-so had happened, I should have done so-and-so," or, "If I had married so-and-so, I suppose I should have had a totally different life." Somehow or other, though, you would always find your way to your own pattern, because I am sure you *are* following a pattern: your pattern of your life. You can embellish your pattern, or you can scamp it, but it is *your* pattern and so long as you are following it you will know harmony, and a mind at ease with itself.

I don't suppose I was at Miss Guyer's more than a year and a half; after that my mother had another idea. With her usual suddenness she explained that I was now going to Paris. She would let Ashfield for the winter, we would go to Paris; I might perhaps start at the same pension at which my sister had been, and see how I liked it.

Everything went according to plan; Mother's arrangements always did. She carried them out with the utmost efficiency, and bent everyone to her will. An excellent let was obtained for the house; Mother and I packed all our trunks (I don't know that there were quite so many round-topped monsters as there had been when we went to the south of France, but there were still a goodly number), and in next to no time we were settled in the Hotel d'Iena, in the avenue d'Iena in Paris.

Mother was laden with letters of introduction and the addresses of various pensionnats and schools, teachers and advisers of all kinds. She had things sorted out before long. She heard that Madge's pensionnat had changed its character and gone downhill as the years passed—Mademoiselle T. herself had either given up or was about to give up, so my mother merely said we could try it for a bit, and see. This attitude towards schooling would hardly be approved of nowadays, but to my mother trying a school was exactly like trying a new restaurant. If you looked inside you couldn't tell what it was like; you must try it, and if you didn't like it the sooner you moved from it the better. Of course then you had not to bother with G.C.E. School Certificate, O levels, A levels and serious thoughts for the future.

I started at Mademoiselle T.'s, and stayed there for about two months, until the end of the term. I was fifteen. My sister had distinguished herself on arriving, when she was dared by some other girl to jump out of a window. She had immediately done so—and arrived slap in the middle of a teatable round which Mademoiselle T. and distinguished parents were sitting. "What hoydens these English girls are!" exclaimed Mademoiselle T. in high displeasure. The girls who egged her on were maliciously pleased, but they admired her for her feat.

My entry was not at all sensational. I was merely a quiet mouse. By the third day I was in misery with homesickness. In the last four or five years I had been so closely attached to my mother, hardly ever leaving her, that it was not unnatural that the first time I really went away from her I should feel homesick. The curious thing was that I didn't know what was the matter with me. I just didn't want to eat. Every time I thought of my mother, tears came into my eyes and ran down my cheeks. I remember looking at a blouse which Mother had made —extremely badly—with her own fingers, and the fact that it *was* made badly, that it did not fit, that the tucks were uneven, made me cry all the more. I managed to conceal these feelings from the outside world, and only wept at night into my pillow. When my mother came to fetch me the following Sunday I greeted her as usual, but when we got back to the hotel I burst into tears and flung my arms round her neck. I am glad to say that at least I did not ask her to take me away; I knew quite well that I had to stop there. Besides, having seen Mother I felt that I wasn't going to be homesick any more; I knew what was the matter with me.

I had no recurrence of homesickness. Indeed, I now enjoyed my days at Mademoiselle T.'s very much. There were French girls, American girls and a good many Spanish and Italian girls—not many English. I liked the company of the American girls especially. They had a breezy interesting way of talking and reminded me of my Cauterets friend, Marguerite Prestley.

I can't remember much about the work side of things—I don't think it can have been very interesting. In history we seemed to be doing the period of the Fronde, which I knew pretty well from the reading of historical novels; and in geography I have been mystified for life by learning the provinces of France as they were in the time of the Fronde rather than as they are now. We also learned the names of the months as they were during the French Revolution. My faults in French dictation horrified the mistress in charge so much she could hardly believe it. "*Vraiment, c'est impossible,*" she said. "*Vous, qui parles si bien le français, vous avez fait vingt-cinq fautes en dictés, vingt-cinq!*"

Nobody else had made more than five. I was quite an interesting phenomenon by reason of my failure. I suppose it was natural enough under the circumstances, since I had known French entirely by talking it. I spoke it colloquially but of course, entirely by ear, and the words *été* and *était* sounded exactly the same to me: I spelled it one way or the other purely by chance, hoping I might have hit upon the right one. In some French subjects, literature, recitation, and so on, I was in the top class; as regards French grammar and spelling I was practically in the bottom class. It made it difficult for my poor teachers—and I suppose shaming for me—except that I can't feel that I really *cared.*

I was taught the piano by an elderly lady called Madame Legrand. She had been there for a great many years. Her favourite method of teaching the piano was to play *à quatre mains* with her pupil. She was insistent on pupils being taught to read music. I was not bad at reading music, but playing it with Madame Legrand was something of an ordeal. We both sat on the benchlike music seat and, as Madame Legrand was extremely well covered, she took up the greater part of it and elbowed me away from the middle of the piano. She played with great vigour, using her elbows, which stuck out slightly akimbo, the result being that the unfortunate person who was playing the other two hands had to play with one elbow stuck tightly to her side.

With a certain natural craftiness I managed nearly always to play the *bass* side of the duet. Madame Legrand was led into this the more easily because she so enjoyed her own performance, and naturally the treble gave her a far better chance of pouring her soul into the music. Sometimes for quite a long time, owing to the vigour of her playing and her absorption in it, she failed to realize that I had lost my place in the bass. Sooner or later I hesitated over a bar, got one behind, tried to catch up, not sure where I was, and then tried to play such notes as would accord with what Madame Legrand was playing. Since, however, we were reading music I could not always anticipate this intelligently. Suddenly, as the hideous cacophony we were making dawned upon her, she would stop, raise her hands in the air and exclaim: "*Mais qu'est-ce que vous jouez là, petite? Que c'est horrible!*" I couldn't have agreed with her more—horrible it was. We would then start again at the beginning. Of course, if I was playing the treble my lack of coordination was noticed at once. However, as a whole, we got on well. Madame Legrand puffed and snorted a great deal the whole time she played. Her bosom rose and fell, groans sometimes came from her, it was alarming but fascinating. She also smelled rather high, which was not so fascinating.

There was to be a concert at the end of the term, and I was scheduled to play two pieces, one the third movement from the *Sonata Pathétique* of Beethoven, and the other a piece called *Serenade d'Aragone*, or something like that. I took a scunner to the *Serenade d'Aragone* straight away. I found extra-ordinary difficulty in playing it—I don't know why; it was certainly much easier than the Beethoven. Though my playing of the Beethoven came on well, the *Serenade d'Aragone* continued to be a very poor performance. I practised it ardently but I seemed to make myself even more nervous. I woke up at night, thinking I was playing, and all sorts of things would happen. The notes of the piano would stick, and I would find I was playing an organ instead of the piano, or I was late in arriving, or the concert had taken place the night before. . . . It all seems so silly when one remembers it.

Two days before the concert I had such high fever that they sent for my mother. The doctor could find no cause for it. However, he gave it as his view that it would be much better if I did not play at the concert, and if I were removed from the school for two or three days until the concert was over. I cannot tell you of my thankfulness, though at the same time I had the feeling of somebody who has failed at something they had been determined to accomplish.

I remember now that at an arithmetic exam at Miss Guyer's school I had come out bottom, though I had been top of the class all the week previously. Somehow, when I read the questions at the exam my mind shut up and I was unable to think.

There are people who can pass exams, often high up, after being almost bottom in class; there are people who can perform in public much better than they perform in private; and there are people who are just the opposite. I was one of the bottom. It is obvious that I chose the right career. The most blessed thing about being an author is that you do it in private and *in your own time*. It can worry you, bother you, give you a headache; you can go nearly mad trying to arrange your plot in the way it should go and you know it could go; *but*—you do not have to stand up and make a fool of yourself in public.

I returned to the pensionnat with great relief and in good spirits. Immediately I tried to see if I could now play the *Serenade d'Aragone*. I certainly played it better than I had ever done before, but the performance was still poor. I went on learning the rest of the Beethoven sonata with Madam Legrand, who, though disappointed in me as a pupil who might have done her credit, was still kind and encouraging and said I had a proper sense of music.

The two winters and one summer that I spent in Paris were some of the happiest days I have known. All sorts of delightful things happened all the time. Some American friends of my grandfather whose daughter sang in Grand Opera, lived there. I went to hear her as Marguerite in *Faust*. At the pensionnat, they did not take girls to hear *Faust*—the subject was not supposed to be "*convenable*" for "*les jeunes filles*." "I think people tended to be rather optimistic over the easy corruption of *les jeunes filles;* you would have to have far more knowledge than *jeunes filles* did in those days to know anything improper was going on at Marguerite's window. I never understood in Paris why Marguerite was suddenly in her prison. Had she, I wondered, stolen the jewellery? Certainly pregnancy and the death of the child never even occurred to me.

We were taken mostly to the Opéra Comique. *Thaïs, Werther, Carmen, La Bohème, Manon. Werther* was my favourite. At the Grand Opera House I heard *Tannhaüser*, as well as *Faust*.

Mother took me to dressmakers, and I began to appreciate clothes for the first time. I had a pale grey crepe de chine semi-evening dress made, which filled me with joy—I had never had anything so grown-up looking before. It was sad that my bosom was still uncooperative, so that I had to have a lot of ruffles of crepe de chine hurriedly tucked into the bodice, but I was still hopeful that one day a couple of truly womanly bosoms, firm, round and large, would be mine. How lucky that vision into the future is spared to us.

Otherwise I should have seen myself at thirty-five, with a round womanly bosom well developed, but, alas, everybody else going about with chests as flat as boards, and if they *were* so unfortunate as to have bosoms, tightening them out of existence.

Through the introductions mother had brought, we went into French society. American girls were welcomed always to the Faubourg St. Germain and it was acceptable for the sons of the French aristocracy to marry rich Americans. Though I was far from rich, my father was known to have been American, and all Americans were supposed to have some money. It was a curious, decorous old-world society.

The Frenchmen I met were polite, very *comme il faut* and nothing could have been duller from a girl's point of view. However, I learned French phraseology of the politest kind. I also learned dancing and deportment, with someone called, I think (though it seems improbable), Mr. Washington Lob. Mr. Washington Lob was the closest thing to Mr. Turveydrop that I can imagine. I learned the Washington Post, the Boston and a few other things, and I also learned the various ranges of cosmopolitan society. "Suppose now, you were about to sit down by an elderly married lady. How would you sit?" I looked at Mr. Washington Lob with blank eyes. "I should—er—sit," I said puzzled.

"Show me." He had some gilt chairs there, and I sat down in a gilt chair, trying to hide my legs as much as possible underneath the chair.

"No, no, that is impossible. That will never do," said Mr. Washington Lob. "You turn slightly sideways, that is enough, not more; and as you sit down you are leaning slightly to the right, so you bend your left knee slightly, so that it is almost like a little bow as you sit." I had to practise this a good deal.

The only things I really hated were my drawing and painting lessons. Mother was adamant on that subject; she would *not* let me off: "Girls should be able to do water colours."

So very rebelliously, twice a week, I was called for by a suitable young woman (since girls did not go about alone in Paris) and taken by métro or bus to an atelier somewhere near the flower market. There I joined a class of young ladies, painting violets in a glass of water, lilies in ajar, daffodils in a black vase. There would be terrific sighs as the lady in charge came round. *"Mais vous ne voyez rien,"* she said to me. "First you must start with the *shadows:* do you not see? Here, and here, and *here* there are shadows."

But I never saw the shadows; all I saw were some violets in a glass of water. Violets were all over. I could match the shade of mauve on my palette, and I would then paint the violets a flat mauve. I quite agree that the result did not look like a bunch of violets in a glass of water, but I did not see, and I don't think have ever seen, what does make shadows look like a bunch of violets in water. On some days, to ease my depression, I would draw the table legs or an odd chair in perspective, which cheered me up, but which did not go down at all well with my instructress. Though I met many charming Frenchmen, strangely enough I did not fall in love with any of them. Instead I conceived a passion for the reception clerk in the hotel, Monsieur Strie. He was tall and thin, rather like a tapeworm, with pale blond hair and a tendency to spots. I really cannot understand what I saw in him. I never had the courage to speak to him, though he occasionally said *"Bonjour, Mademoiselle"* as I passed through the hall. It was difficult to have fantasies about Monsieur Strie. I imagined myself sometimes nursing him through the plague in French Indo-China, but it took much effort to keep that vision going. As he finally gasped out his last breath he would murmur, "Mademoiselle, I always adored you in the days at the hotel"—which was all right as far as it went, but when I noticed Monsieur Strie writing industriously behind the desk the following day it seemed to me extremely unlikely that he would ever say such a thing, even on his deathbed.

We passed the Easter holidays going on expeditions to Versailles, Fontainebleau, and various other places, and then, with her usual suddenness, Mother announced that I should not be returning to Mademoiselle T.'s.

"I don't think much of that place," she said. "No interesting teaching. It's not what it was in Madge's time. I am going back to England, and I have arranged that you shall go to Miss Hogg's school at Auteuil, Les Marroniers."

I can't remember feeling anything beyond mild surprise. I had enjoyed myself at Mademoiselle T.'s, but I didn't particularly want to go back there. In fact it seemed more interesting to go to a new place. I don't know whether it was stupidity on my part or amiability—I like to think, of course, that it was the latter—but I was always prepared to like the next thing that came along.

So I went to Les Marroniers, which was a good school but extremely English. I enjoyed it, but found it dull. I had quite a good music teacher, but not as much fun as Madame Legrand had been. As everyone talked English all the time, in spite of the fact that it was strictly forbidden, nobody learned much French.

Outside activities were not encouraged, or indeed perhaps even allowed, at Les Marroniers, so at last I was to shake myself free of my detested painting and drawing lessons. The only thing I missed was passing through the flower market, which really had been heavenly. It was no surprise to me at the end of the summer holidays when my mother suddenly said to me at Ashfield that I was not going back to Les Marroniers. She had had a new idea for my education.

V

Grannie's doctor, Dr. Barwood, had a sister-in-law who kept a small establishment for "finishing" girls in Paris. She only took twelve to fifteen girls, and they were all studying music or taking courses at the Conservatoire or the Sorbonne. "How did I like that idea?" my mother asked. As I have said, I welcomed new ideas; in fact my motto might have been established by then as "Try anything once." So in the autumn I went to Miss Dryden's establishment just off the Arc de Triomphe in the Avenue du Bois.

Being at Miss Dryden's suited me down to the ground. For the first time I felt that what we were doing was really interesting. There were twelve of us. Miss Dryden herself was tall, rather fierce, with beautifully arranged white hair, an excellent figure, and a red nose, which she was in the habit of rubbing violently when she was angry. She had a dry, ironic form of conversation that was alarming but stimulating. Assisting her was a French coadjutor, Madame Petit. Madame Petit was very French, temperamental, highly emotional, remarkably unfair, and we were all devoted to her, and not nearly so much in awe of her as we were of Miss Dryden.

It was, of course, much more like living in a family, but a serious attitude was taken towards our studies. There was an emphasis on music, but we had plenty of interesting classes of all kinds. We had people from the Comédie Française, who gave us talks on Molière, Racine and Corneille, and singers from the Conservatoire, who sang the airs of Lully and Gluck. We had a dramatic class where we all recited. Luckily we did not have so many "dictés" here, so my spelling faults were not quite so noticeable, and since my spoken French was better than the others' I enjoyed myself thoroughly reciting the lines of *Andromaque* feeling myself indeed that tragic heroine as I stood and declaimed:

"Seigneur, toutes ces grandeurs ne me touchent plus guère."

I think we all rather enjoyed ourselves at the drama class. We were taken to the Comédie Française and saw the classic dramas and several modern plays as well. I saw Sarah Bernhardt in what must have been one of the last roles of her career, as the golden pheasant in Rostand's *Chantecler*. She was old, lame, feeble, and her golden voice was cracked, but she was certainly a great actress, she held you with her impassioned emotion. Even more exciting than Sarah Bernhardt did I find Réjane. I saw her in a modern play, *La Course aux Flambeaux*. She had a wonderful power of making you reel, behind a hard repressed manner: the existence of a tide of feeling and emotion which she would never allow to come out into the open. I can still hear now, as I sit quiet a minute or two with my eyes closed, her voice, and see her face in the last words of the play, "*Pour sauver ma fille, j'ai tué ma mère*," and the deep thrill this sent through one as the curtain came down.

It seems to me that teaching can only be satisfactory if it awakens some response in you. Mere information is no good, it gives you nothing more than you had before. To be talked to about plays by *actresses*, repeating words and speeches from them; to have real singers singing you *Bois Épais* or an aria from Gluck's *Orphée* was to bring to life in you a passionate love of the art you were hearing. It opened a new world to me, a world in which I have been able to live ever since.

My own serious study was music, of course, both singing and piano. I studied the piano with an Austrian, Charles Fürster. He occasionally came to London and gave recitals. He was a good but frightening teacher. His method was to wander round the room as you played. He had the air of not listening, looked out of the window, smelled a flower, but all of a sudden, as you played a false note or phrased something badly, he would swing round with the alacrity of a pouncing tiger and cry out: "*Hein, qu'est-ce que vous jouez là, petite, hein? C'est atroce.*" It was shattering to the nerves at first, but one got used to it. He was a passionate addict of Chopin, so that I learned mostly Chopin Etudes and Waltzes, the *Fantaisie Impromptue*, and one of the Ballades. I know I was getting on well under his teaching, and it made me happy. I also learned the Sonatas of Beethoven, as well as several light, what he called "drawing-room pieces," a Romance of Fauré, the Barcarolle of Tchaikovsky, and others. I practised with real assiduity, usually about seven hours a day. I think a wild hope was springing up within me—I don't know that I ever let it quite come into my consciousness, but it was there in the background—that perhaps I could be a pianist, could play at concerts. It would be a long time and hard work, but I knew that I was improving rapidly.

My singing lessons had begun before this period. My teacher was Monsieur Boué. He and Jean de Reszke were supposed at that time to be the two leading singing teachers of Paris. Jean de Reszke had been a famous tenor and Boué an operatic baritone. He lived in an apartment five flights up with no lift. I used to arrive at the fifth storey completely out of breath, as indeed was only natural. The apartments all looked so alike that you lost count of the storeys you had climbed, but you always knew when you were getting to Monsieur Boué's because of the wallpaper on the stairs. On the last turn was an enormous grease mark which had a rough resemblance to the head of a cairn terrier.

When I arrived I would be immediately greeted with reproaches. What did I mean by breathing fast like that? Why did I have to be out of breath? Someone my age should spring upstairs, without panting. Breathing was everything. "Breathing is the whole of singing, you should know that by now." He would then reach for his tape measure, which was always at hand. This he would put round my diaphragm and then urge me to breathe in, hold it, and then breathe out as completely as possible. He would calculate the difference between the two measurements, nodding his head occasionally and saying: "*C'est bien, c'est bien*, it advances. You have a good chest, an excellent chest. You have splendid expansion, and what is more, I will tell you something, you will never have the consumption. That is a sad thing for some singers; they get the consumption, but with you no. As long as you practise your breathing, all will be well with you. You like beefsteak?" I said yes, I was extremely fond of beefsteak. "That is good too; that is the best food for a singer. You cannot eat large meals, or eat often, but I say to my opera singers you will have at three o'clock in the afternoon a large steak and a glass of stout; after that *nothing* till you sing at nine o'clock."

We then proceeded to the singing lesson proper. The *voix de tête*, he said, was very good, it was perfect, properly produced and natural, and my chest notes were not too bad; but the *médium*, the *médium* was extremely weak. So to begin with I was to sing mezzo-soprano songs to develop *le médium*. At intervals he would get exasperated with what he called my English face. "English faces," he said, "have no expression! They are not mobile. The skin round the mouth, it does not move; and the voice, the words, everything, they come from the back of the throat. That is very bad. The French language has got to come from the *palate*, from the roof of the mouth. The roof of the mouth, the bridge of the nose, *that* is where the voice of the *médium* comes from. You speak French very well, very fluently, though it is unfortunate you have not the English accent but the accent of the Midi. Why do you have the accent of the Midi?"

I thought for a minute, and then I said perhaps because I had learned French from a French maid who had come from Pau.

"Ah, that explains it," he said. "Yes, that is it. It is the accent *méridional* that you have. As I say, you speak French fluently, but you speak it as though it were English because you speak it from the back of your throat. You must move your lips. Keep your teeth close together, but move your *lips*. Ah, I know what we shall do."

He would then tell me to stick a pencil in the corner of my mouth and articulate as well as possible while I was singing, without letting the pencil drop out. It was extraordinarily difficult at first, but in the end I managed it. My teeth clamped the pencil and my lips then had to move a great deal to make the words come out at all.

Boué's fury was great one day when I brought in the air from *Samson et Delilah*, "*Mon coeur s'ouvre à ta voix*," and asked him if I could possibly learn it, as I had enjoyed the opera so much.

"But what is this you have here?" he said, looking at the piece of music. "What is this? What key is it in? It is in a transposed key."

I said I had bought the version for a soprano voice.

He shouted with rage: "But Delilah is not a soprano part. It is a mezzo part. Do you not know that if you sing an air from an opera, it must always be sung in the key it was written in? You cannot transpose for a soprano voice what has been written for a mezzo voice—it puts the whole emphasis wrong. Take it away. If you bring it in the proper mezzo key, yes, you shall learn it."

I never dared sing a transposed song again.

I learned large quantities of French songs, and a lovely Ave Maria of Cherubini's. We debated for some time how I was to pronounce the Latin of that. "The English pronounce Latin in the Italian way, the French have their own way of pronouncing Latin. I think, since you are English, you had better sing it in the Italian pronunciation."

I also sang a good many of Schubert's songs in German. In spite of not knowing German this was not too difficult; and I sang songs in Italian, of course. On the whole I was not allowed to be too ambitious, but after about six months or so of study I was allowed to sing the aria from *La Bohème*, "*Che gelida manina*," and also the aria from *Tosca*, "*Vissi d'arte*."

It was indeed a happy time.

Sometimes, after a visit to the Louvre, we were taken to have tea at Rumpelmayer's. There could be no delight in life for a greedy girl like tea at Rumpelmayer's. My favourites were those glorious cakes with cream and marron piping of a sickliness which was incomparable.

We were taken, of course, for walks in the Bois—a very fascinating place. One day, I remember, when we were going in a neat crocodile, two by two, along a deeply wooded path, a man came out from behind some trees— a classic case of indecent exposure. We must all have seen him, I think, but we all behaved in a decorous manner as if we had noticed nothing unusual— possibly we may have been not quite sure of what it was we *had* seen. Miss Dryden, herself, who was in charge of us that day, sailed along with the iron-clad belligerence of a battleship. We followed her. I suppose the man, whose upper half was very correct, with black hair and pointed beard and a very smart cravat and tie, must have spent his day wandering about the darker places of the Bois so as to surprise decorous young ladies from pensionnats, walking in a crocodile, wishing perhaps to add to their knowledge of life in Paris. I may add that, as far as I know, not one of us mentioned this incident to any of the other girls; there was not so much as a giggle. We were all splendidly modest in those days.

We had occasional parties at Miss Dryden's, and on one occasion a former pupil of hers, an American woman now married to a French Vicomte, arrived with her son, Rudy. Rudy might have been a French baron, but in appearance he was a thoroughly American college boy. He must have blanched a little at the sight of twelve nubile girls looking at him with interest, approbation, and possible romance in their eyes.

"I've got my work cut out shaking hands round here," he declared in a cheerful voice. We all met Rudy again the next day at the Palais de Glace, where some of us were skating and some learning to skate. Rudy was again determinedly gallant, anxious not to let his mother down. He skated several circuits of the rink with those of us who were able to stand up. I, as so often in these matters, was unlucky. I had only just begun to learn, and on my first afternoon had succeeded in throwing the skating instructor. This, I may say, had made him extremely angry, He had been held up to the ridicule of his colleagues. He prided himself on being able to hold up *anyone*, even the stoutest American lady, and to be floored by a tall thin girl must have infuriated him. He took me out for my turn as seldom as possible after this. Anyway I didn't think I would risk being pioneered by Rudy round the rink—I should probably throw *him*, too, and then *he* would have been annoyed.

Something happened to me at the sight of Rudy. We only saw him on those few occasions, but they marked a point of transition. From that moment forward I stepped out of the territory of hero worship. All the romantic love I had felt for people real and unreal—people in books, people in the public eye, actual people who came to the house—finished at that moment. I no longer had the capacity for selfless love or the wish to sacrifice myself on their behalf. From that day I began to think of young men only as young men—exciting creatures whom I would enjoy meeting, and among whom, some day, I should find my husband (Mr. Right in fact). I did not fall in love with Rudy—perhaps I might have, if I had met him often—but I did suddenly feel *different*. I had become one of the world of females on the prowl! From that moment, the image of the Bishop of London, who had been my last object of hero worship, faded from my mind. I wanted to meet *real* young men, *lots* of real young men—in fact there couldn't be too many of them.

I am hazy now as to how long I remained at Miss Dryden's—a year, perhaps eighteen months, I do not think as long as two years. My volatile mother did not propose any further changes of educational plan: perhaps she did not hear of anything that excited her. But I think really that she had an intuitive knowledge that I had found what satisfied me. I was learning things that mattered, that built themselves into me as part of an interest in life.

One dream of mine faded before I left Paris. Miss Dryden was expecting an old pupil of hers, the Countess of Limerick, who herself was a very fine pianist, a pupil of Charles Fürster's. Usually the two or three girls who were studying the piano would give an informal concert on these occasions. I was one of them. The result was catastrophic. I was nervous beforehand, but not unusually so, no more than would be natural, but as soon as I sat down at the piano inefficiency overwhelmed me like a tide. I played wrong notes, my tempo went, my phrasing was amateur and hamhanded—I was just a mess.

Nobody could have been kinder than Lady Limerick. She talked to me later and said she had realized how nervous I had been, and that one did get these fits of what really qualified as stage fright. Perhaps I would get over them later when I became more experienced in playing before an audience. I was grateful for those kind words, but I knew myself that there was more to it than that.

I continued to study, but before I finally went home I asked Charles Fürster frankly whether he thought that by hard work and application I could one day be a professional pianist. He, too, was kind, but he told me no lies. He said that he thought I had not the temperament to play in public, and I knew he was right. I was grateful to him for telling me the truth. I was miserable about it for a while, but I tried hard not to dwell on it more than I could help.

If the thing you want beyond anything cannot be, it is much better to recognize it and go forward, instead of dwelling on one's regrets and hopes. Such a rebuff coming early helped me for the future; it taught me that I had not the kind of temperament for exhibition of any kind. I can describe what it seemed like by saying that I could not control my *physical* reaction.

JULIAN SYMONS

Foreword: A Portrait of Agatha Christie

When Agatha Christie died in January 1976, she was undoubtedly the most famous detective story writer in the world. In Britain alone all of her most popular titles sold in millions; in the United States they were almost equally successful; and in every European country her name was a household word. Her fame even extended to the heart of the Soviet bloc: an edition of some books published in Moscow sold out immediately.

The personality behind the creation of Hercule Poirot and Miss Marple was that of a shy and in most ways very conventional middle-class English lady. Agatha Mary Clarissa Miller was born in the Devonshire seaside resort of Torquay in 1890, the third child of a well-to-do American father and a mother who was markedly sensitive and aesthetically perceptive. In her charming autobiography Agatha gives very clear sketches of them both, her father an idle but agreeable man, her mother almost clairvoyant at times, and a person who saw life and people in colors that "were always slightly at variance with reality." Perhaps this is the quality she passed on most directly to Agatha, the romantic tendency to see everything a little bigger than life-size, to be fascinated by the mysterious and strange, and to weave stories that explained the strangeness.

There was nothing unusual about Agatha Miller's childhood, except that she never went to school. She was taught at home by her mother, and at

From *The New Bedside, Bathtub & Armchair Companion to Agatha Christie*, edited by Dick Riley and Pam McAllister. © 1979 by Ungar Publishing Company.

times by governesses, and evolved elaborate games that she played by herself, games in which one can perhaps see the germ of the intricate plots she evolved in later years. In adolescence, like other young girls of her class and time, she went to dances (never unaccompanied, because "you did not go to a dance alone with a young man") where she found difficulty in managing her programme so that she danced with the right young man. She flirted, had proposals, and in 1914 married dashing Archie Christie, who became one of the first pilots in the Royal Flying Corps during World War I.

Agatha worked in a hospital and eventually found herself an assistant in the dispensary. There she conceived the idea of writing a detective story, something she had been challenged to do a year or two earlier by her elder sister Madge. Since she was surrounded by poisons, what more natural than that this should be a poisoning case. What kind of plot should it be? "The whole point of a *good* detective story was that it must be somebody obvious but at the same time, for some reason, you would then find that it was *not* obvious, that he could not possibly have done it." Readers of her first detective story, *The Mysterious Affair at Styles*, will remember that this is just what happens in the book.

Then there must be a detective. What should he be like? She was devoted to Sherlock Holmes, but recognised that she must produce a character outside the Holmes pattern. What kind of person? There were a variety of detectives flourishing in English fiction at the time, including the blind Max Carrados, whose sense of smell was so strongly developed that he could discern the spirit gum in a false moustache across a room, and the super-scientific Doctor Thorndyke, but Agatha Christie rightly thought that these were not her kind of detectives. Then she remembered a colony of Belgian refugees who had come to her part of Devon at the beginning of the war. Why not make her a man a retired Belgian police officer? He would be meticulous, a tidy little man, always neat and orderly, with a slight flavour of absurdity about him. Since he was to be small, why not call him Hercules? And then the surname. She did not remember how she found the name Poirot, but it appeared. "It went well not with Hercules but Hercule— Hercule Poirot. That was all right—settled, thank goodness."

Such was the birth of Hercule Poirot. The book was completed in 1915, but had to wait five years for publication. It duly appeared, and although she made little money from it because of the outrageous agreement that she had signed as a raw and innocent author, she felt sufficiently encouraged to start another story.

One of the decisive events in her life was the publication of that first detective story. Another, six years later, was her disappearance for several days. Her car had been abandoned, and the police treated the case as one in which her violent death could not be ruled out. After a nationwide police hunt she was found in a hotel at the spa of Harrogate, in the north of England. It was immediately suggested that her explanation of loss of memory was not correct, and that the disappearance had been a publicity stunt.

What is the truth? Those who read her autobiography in the hope of finding an answer will be disappointed, for she makes no reference to the disappearance. But she does tell us the background of her life immediately before it, and this helps to explain what happened. Her much-loved mother had recently died, and the duty of clearing up everything in the house to which she was deeply attached fell upon Agatha. Her husband had told her that he could not bear illness, death, or indeed any kind of trouble, and there was no question of his staying in Devon with her. Under the stress of living again—and alone—in the house where she had spent an idyllically happy childhood, she broke down. She wept uncontrollably when she could not start the car, and was unable to remember her own name when writing a cheque. Then her husband told her that he was in love with another woman and wanted a divorce. This was the situation at the time of her disappearance. If one wanted a further indication that her story of amnesia was true, it would be in the fact that during her stay in Harrogate she used the name of her husband's mistress.

For two or three years she was deeply unhappy, and although she went on writing, the books she produced are markedly inferior to her best work. Then she met somebody at a dinner party who talked to her about the entrancing quality of Baghdad, and said that she should also look at the archaeological finds recently made at Ur in Mesopotamia. She hurriedly canceled a projected trip to the West Indies and instead took the Orient Express, which went at that time all the way from England. She had a life-long love of trains, feeling that some steam engines were personal friends, and as she says herself, trains and houses were always more real to her than most people.

The trip was eventful. It provided the basis for *Murder on the Orient Express* and for some other books, but something more important than that happened. She was delighted by the beauty of Ur, and on a second trip met a thin, dark young man named Max Mallowan, assistant to Leonard Woolley, who was in charge of the expedition. She went with Max Mallowan to see the desert city of Ukhaidir, and—as he afterward told her—it was when they were stranded in the desert for hours and she made no fuss about it that he decided to propose marriage. They were married in 1930, and it does not seem an exaggeration to say that, in spite of the fact that he was fourteen years her junior, they lived happily ever after. She accompanied him on archaeological digs, and these too provided the background for stories. Max

Mallowan became one of the most distinguished figures in his field. In 1968 he was knighted, and three years later Agatha achieved the prime honour possible to a woman in Britain, when she was made a D.B.E., a Dame of the British Empire.

By the time of her death she had produced more than eighty crime stories, along with half a dozen romantic novels under the name of Mary Westmacott, several plays, some of which she had written herself and some adapted from books and stories by other hands, and two volumes of autobiography.

That is the account of a life, but what was she like as a person? There can be no doubt that the shock of discovering Archie Christie's unfaithfulness and the furor caused by the disappearance changed her. In her autobiographical pages one glimpses a different personality, more casual, reckless, and gay than the Agatha Christie of the 1940s and 1950s. No doubt she had always been different but now she was painfully shy with strangers, and, as she said herself, conversation with her was not easy. She absolutely refused to make speeches now that she was famous, and carried this so far that when she succeeded Dorothy L. Sayers as president of Britain's famous Detection Club, a deputy had to propose toasts and introduce guests.

She particularly disliked being interviewed, especially after one dinner when she chatted in the cloakroom with what seemed a pleasant young woman and found their conversation splashed across a newspaper's gossip page the next day in the form of an interview. She acceded most reluctantly to any request for an interview, and always made a stipulation that no question should be asked about the disappearance. "I cannot say that I look forward to it, but I suppose that as it is you it will be alright," she wrote to me when I suggested that we should have a conversation about crime stories for publication in an English paper. I took a tape recorder with me, but at first it was far from all right. She answered in monosyllables, and I began to despair of her saying anything interesting. It was not until she realised that I was uneasy about whether the machine was recording and too ignorant of its operation to play it back that she relaxed and our conversation began to flow.

Even then she talked little about anything personal, although she spoke freely enough about her writing. Her view of the reasons for the success of the *The Mousetrap* (which has run far longer than any other play in the history of the English theatre) were typically practical. It was a small play in a small theatre, which meant that the running costs were low, and you could take anybody to it, including children and old ladies. "It is not really frightening, it is not really horrible, it is not really a farce, but is has got a bit of all those things and perhaps that satisfies a lot of different people."

What about Poirot, what did she feel about him? Well, she had lots of letters from people, saying that she must love him. "Little they know. I can't bear him now." Because of her readers' reactions it was impossible to get rid of him, but she much preferred Miss Marple. Had she always wanted to write detective stories? Not particularly, she would have liked to try several different sorts of book. "But of course detective stories supported me and my daughter for years, and they had to be written." And if she had not been a writer? "I might have had a shot at sculpture, but I wouldn't have been any good at it. And, oh yes, I would quite have liked to be a hospital nurse."

So the interview went well, but at the end of it I knew little more about the woman who sat opposite me. At this time she was seventy years old, plump and well preserved, the model of that peculiarly English kind of country lady whom one sees serving tea on a green lawn, attending fêtes to raise funds for the local Conservative party, expressing entirely conventional opinions on almost every subject. And that picture is true enough, for part of her was that English country lady. The problem remains then: how did this perfectly nice conventional Englishwoman, with her fur coat and tweeds, her twin set and pearls, come to write so much about murder?

The answer, I think, is that there existed another and more interesting Agatha Christie. Yes, she was a conventional English woman; but she was also the woman who faced discomfort and danger intrepidly on expeditions with her husband, who thought that a few bites from bedbugs were of no account compared with the pleasures of travel and in particular of long train journeys, and who said that the best breakfast in the world was not a meal served off silverplate in a grand hotel but sausages cooked on a primus stove in the desert. Yes, her conversation was mostly commonplace, but behind it rioted an immensely ingenious, subtle, and one must say, potentially criminal imagination. In at least one real-life murder case the murderer had been influenced by an Agatha Christie story.

As a detective story writer her works belonged firmly to the world in which she had been brought up. No unpleasant physical details were allowed to enter her books, and we are not meant to feel any emotional involvement in relation to the body in the library or on the links. Her supreme skill was in the construction of plot, and she has never been excelled as a creator of deceptive puzzles, the kind in which through something said or something seen we are given a clue. If this clue is interpreted correctly it will tell us a murderer's identity, but if we make one of half a dozen other more obvious interpretations it will mislead us. A witness says what she has seen, and she is a witness of truth, but is it physically possible for her to have seen it? A remark is made that seems damning evidence against one character, but look

at the remark again and it may point to another. We are told that a list of articles belonging to passengers on a plane will help us to solve a crime and so
it may, but we are likely to look for the wrong article.

It would seem that Agatha Christie had this kind of skill right from that
splendid beginning with *The Mysterious Affair at Styles*, which is not to say
that her books are even in merit. There is general agreement, although she
would not have shared it, that the forty-odd Poirot books are better than the
much smaller number featuring Miss Marple, and that the thrillers in which
Tommy and Tuppence appear are inferior tales of a kind not suited to the
Christie talent. It is accepted also that her work showed a decline from the
middle fifties onwards that became steep towards the end of her life. When
this has been said, however, there remain thirty or more books that are brilliant exercises in deception. Which are the best of these?

A list of my own dozen favorite Christie's would certainly be headed by
The Murder of Roger Ackroyd, which remains the best shock ending of all time
and shows that as early as 1926 her mastery of her chosen form was
complete. From the same decade I should choose also *The Mysterious Affair
at Styles* and *The Man in the Brown Suit*, in which the Ackroyd trick was given
a preliminary airing. The thirties was not only her most prolific but also her
finest decade, including a whole series of marvellously-plotted books: *Peril at
End House, Thirteen at Dinner, The A.B.C. Murders, Death in the Air, Death on
the Nile*, and in 1939 the book that I would place second only to *Roger
Ackroyd, Ten Little Indians*.

And the Christie level is almost as high in the forties. There is a poison
story, *Sad Cypress* (she made considerable and varied use of her veneniferous
knowledge), the unusually sinister *Towards Zero*, and *Death Comes As the End*,
a *tour de force* set in ancient Egypt.

There is my dozen, but I must make room for a couple more, one from
the fifties and one from the sixties. *What Mrs. McGillicuddy Saw!* is, for me,
the most cunning of the Miss Marple stories, and *The Pale Horse* of 1961 is
notable as the book in which the murder method—poisoning again—was
actually used in really life.

What is the basis of her lasting attraction? In the years before her death
she was rightly acknowledged as the queen of the Golden Age detective
story, the puzzle pure and complex. She never thought of herself as a great
or even a good writer, but she was the master conjurer of our time. That
conjurer's sleight of hand, the infinitely various tricks of this Cleopatra of old
Thames, will keep her best work fresh and fascinating to each new generation of readers as long as detective stores are read.

PAM McALLISTER

The Impact of Gender on Agatha and Her Craft

"Alas! a woman that attempts the pen, Such a presumptuous creature is esteemed, The fault can by no virture be redeemed." So said Lady Winchilsea, a poet and noblewoman born in 1661.

But surely things had changed on planet earth by the time Agatha took up her pen in the early twentieth century, no? Well, not so much as one might have hoped. Women writers were still fighting the image of being "presumptuous creatures," and worried about being taken seriously.

Agatha was tempted to hide behind a male pseudonym in order to be taken seriously at first. She especially liked the sound of something like "Martin West." "I had the idea that a woman's name would prejudice people against my work, especially in detective stories; that Martin West would be more manly and forthright."

In her forties, with more than ten books published and her fame international, Agatha wanted nothing of being a creature as "presumptuous" as a woman *writer.*

> I wrote things—yes—books and stories. . . . But never, when I was filling in a form and came to the line asking for occupation, would it have occurred to me to fill it in with anything but the time-honoured "married woman."

From *The New Bedside, Bathtub & Armchair Companion to Agatha Christie*, edited by Dick Riley and Pam McAllister. © 1979 by Ungar Publishing Company.

This statement echoed an earlier sentiment held by the eleven-year-old Agatha on the occasion of her first published work, a poem about trams.

> I was elated at seeing myself in print, but I cannot say that it led me to contemplate a literary career.
>
> In fact I only contemplated one thing—a happy marriage. About that I had complete self-assurance—as all my friends did.

After writing her first three books, Agatha was tempted to consider herself a writer, but even this thought was couched in appropriately feminine self-depreciation. She wrote in her autobiography. "It was by now just beginning to dawn on me that perhaps I might be a writer by profession. I was not sure of it yet. I still had an idea that writing books was only the natural successor to embroidering sofa cushions."

In her famed 1929 essay, "A Room of One's Own," feminist author Virginia Woolf prescribed the special requirements needed to encourage women writers: "a woman must have money and a room of her own if she is to write fiction." We might assume that Agatha Christie always had the money and the room if not a number of them, but she claimed at one point not to need a room of her own at all. Indeed, if Agatha had written Virginia Woolf's brave essay, she might have titled it "A *Table* of One's Own."

> I never had a definite place which was *my* room or where I retired specially to write. . . . All I needed was a steady table and a typewriter . . . A marble-topped bedroom washstand table made a good place to write; the dinning-room table between meals was also suitable.

Agatha did have to fight for a table of her own at least once. Accompanying her second husband, Max Mallowan, on an archeological expedition to Nineveh, she encountered Dr. Campbell-Thompson who, it seems from the following account, might well have considered Agatha a "presumptuous creature."

> All I wanted was to buy myself a table in the bazaar. . . . What I *had* to have, if I was going to do my own work, was a solid table at which I could typewrite, and under which I could get my knees. . . . C.T. . . . looked down on me for being willing to spend money on something not absolutely necessary . . .
>
> Writing books, I pointed out, was my work, and I had to have certain tools for it: a typewriter, a pencil, and a table at which I could sit. So C.T. gave way, but he was sad about it.

Eventually, Agatha did want a *room* of her own while on another expedition, this one at Nimrud where she wrote her autobiography. "I petitioned to be allowed to have a small room added on of my own. This I would pay for myself. So, for fifty pounds, I built on a small, square, mud-brick room, and it was there that I began writing this book."

She had come a long way in accepting her identity as a writer by the time she got that room. But don't be fooled. Agatha never rejected the lessons she had learned as a girl, nor rejected the tradition of playing the game talented, spirited woman of her day had to play in this man's world. The game allowed for certain idiosyncrasies—even, in Agatha's case, a fancy for playing the boy's part in youthful theater productions. "We went through the Sleeping Beauty, Cinderella, Beauty and the Beast and so forth. I was fondest of the part of principal boy."

Such playacting, however, never slipped over into Agatha's idea of how women's lives were meant to be shaped. "*You didn't know what was going to happen to you.* That was what made being a woman so exciting. No worry about what you should be or do—Biology would decide. You were waiting for The Man, and when the man came, he would change your life!"

Cherishing this point of view, Agatha lamented the changes that were redefining the traditionally strict gender roles.

> The position of women, over the years, has definitely changed for the worse . . . We have clamoured to be allowed to work as men work. . . .
>
> It seems sad that having established ourselves so cleverly as the "weaker sex," we should now be broadly on a par with the women of primitive tribes who toil in the fields all day.

Indeed, she applauded the ways women had been taught to manipulate men to get their way.

> You've got to hand it to Victorian women, they got their menfolk where they wanted them. They established their frailty, delicacy, sensibility—their constant need of being protected and cherished. . . . All my grandmother's friends seem to me in retrospect singularly resilient and almost invariably successful in getting their own way. They were tough, self-willed, and remarkably well read and well informed.

Lest we have any doubt that Agatha really meant what she said about the woman's sphere, she stated emphatically (with capital letter and italics no less!): "In one respect man was paramount. He was the Head of the

House. A woman, when she married, accepted as her destiny *his* place in the world and *his* way of life. That seems to me sound sense and the foundation of happiness."

It was Agatha's good fortune to have a childhood filled with clever, strong women for models. And she had great admiration for them. Her mother was "an enigmatic and arresting personality—more forceful than my father." Her beloved Nursie was described as "the outstanding figure in my early life" and "the rock of stability."

There was Marie, Agatha's agreeable French governess and Jane, the cook, "who ruled the kitchen with the calm superiority of a queen." And there were family friends. "My mother's nicest friend was Pussy Richards, who often came to stay. She had short hair that curled all over her head, wore manly coats and white shirts, and she was heaven to play with. . . . She led a very adventurous life . . . taking all sorts of different jobs."

Another friend was Lilian Pirie, described by Agatha as "one of the most outstanding personalities I have ever known. . . . There was something faintly awe-inspiring in her . . . and I knew her up to the age of eighty–odd when she died. All that time my admiration and respect for her increased."

The men in Agatha's life were less consistently inspiring. Archie Christie, for example, was sometimes supportive. Of him she wrote, "He always took it for granted that I could do things about which I myself had a good deal of doubt. 'Of course you can do it,' he would say." He taught Agatha to drive, which delighted her no end. "Oh, the joy that car was to me! . . . To be able to go anywhere you chose; to places beyond the reach of your legs; it widened your whole horizon."

Archie was less than helpful, however, when it came to Agatha's writing. In fact he was downright harmful.

> Occasionally I felt the urge to outline to him some idea I had for a new story, or the plot of a new book. When I had described it haltingly, it sounded, even to my ears, extraordinarily banal, futile and a great many other adjectives which I will not particularize. . . . "Do you think it will be all right?" "Well, I suppose it might be," said Archie, in a completely damping manner. "It doesn't seem to have much *story* to it, does it?" That plot thereupon fell dead, slain forever.

Max Mallowan was more consistently supportive and encouraging, though he could not bring himself to read his wife's books, which must at least have *felt* like a lack of appreciation. Nevertheless, Agatha insisted that, as she was a "lowbrow" and Max a "highbrow," they complemented each other nicely.

Such support from her husband notwithstanding, Agatha definitely drew strength from the women in her life—including some imaginary female friends, created in childhood, who stayed with her always. Deprived of attending school, she had populated a make-believe classroom with these friends—clever Ethel Smith with a great mane of hair; Annie Gray, pale, shy, and nervous; beautiful but "worldly" Isabella Sullivan whom Agatha actually disliked; Irish Elsie Green who was poor and wore Isabel's castoff clothes; conscientious, dull Ella White with the bushy hair; and Sue de Verte who Agatha supposed was really herself.

With remarkable candor, Agatha, at age seventy–five, wrote:

> Even now, sometimes, as I put away a dress in a cupboard, I say to myself: "Yes, that would do well for Elsie, green was always her colour." . . . It makes me laugh when I do it, but there "the girls" *are* still, though, unlike me, they have not grown old.

ROBERT BARNARD

Counsel for the Defense

Everyone who reads the traditional type of detective story, whether casually or addictively, will be familiar with the sort of objection to Agatha
Christie and her kind voiced by Edmund Wilson, Bernard Levin and others,
for they are only rehearsing the kind of argument heard over and over from
people who do not respond to the appeal of the mystery story and are bewildered or irritated by their immunity. Most enthusiasts are somewhat at a loss
as to how to counter such arguments: on the one hand, they sense how difficult it is to defend Christie and her contemporaries on their accusers' chosen
grounds; on the other, they have a vague sense that, however reasonable the
grounds may sound, these accusers are somehow missing the point, and that
the sort of appeal these writers have for an enormous and devoted public
rests on quite different foundations.

This latter feeling is, it seems to me, healthy and right. The attacks do
miss the point, and they miss it very often because they bring to Christie all
the preconceptions about what a novel should be which accumulate in the
minds of those whose reading is mainly in the great eighteenth- and nineteenth-century classics of fiction. What they are saying is that *as novels* these
works are beneath contempt: they look for solidly realized character
drawing, for psychological depth, for evocative descriptions of settings, they
look, even, for some "criticism of life," some statement about the human

condition. And when inevitably they come back empty-handed from their search they come to the conclusion that life is too short to fritter away their time on such a trivial, feebleminded means of wasting time.

But in fact they are like a man who prospects for gold in a coal field. The first thing to get clear, in approaching Agatha Christie and her fellows, is that, by approaching them as novelists and by looking for the same sort of qualities one may hope to find in novels, these critics are making a mistake which prejudices the issue right from the start. Crime writers are not trying to write *Crime and Punishment*. Agatha Christie is a teller of popular tales, and should be judged by criteria appropriate to such a genre.

It is never very sensible to act as an evangelist for the detective story: if someone says, "I've never been able to acquire a taste for crime fiction—who do you recommend I try?" the sensible answer probably is, "Don't bother. If you have tried and you haven't responded, then probably the response isn't in you." The problem, for such readers, is usually that they "can never lose the taste of the construction," as Trollope said of some early examples of the form. And the problem is never likely to be resolved. On the other hand, it is reasonable, I think, to go on to suggest that he ought to try thrillers, or science fiction, or historical romances, or love stories—one or other of the branches of popular fiction. Because it is a pity to have become so sophisticated in one's reading that one can no longer thrill to a line like "Mr Holmes, it was the footprint of a gigantic hound!" or even "With a happy sigh she melted into his arms." Because to have lost the power to make these basic responses is to have lost the elementary response to fiction as *story*.

It is relevant here to look at the approach to the detective story of the French-American critic Jacques Barzun, one of the most voluminous and stimulating writers on the genre. One would like to be able to say one of the most influential as well, but in fact his writings have constituted an example of that most lonely and heroic of struggles—a battle against the fashionable tide. In article after article, and in his extraordinary *Catalogue of Crime*, he has elevated the authors of the classical whodunnit and deplored the shift in critical interest toward the realistic novel of crime—in particular the tough thriller-detective school of Hammett, Chandler and their pale equivalents in Great Britain. Where the critical orthodoxy today is to elevate this group to a lonely eminence, to see in Hammett and Chandler convincing diagnoses of the deep social malaises inherent in American capitalism, to praise the psychological insights of a Highsmith or a Symons, Barzun, in a series of splendid and idiosyncratic tirades, dissents: "the genre has not grown up, has not 'become literature': it has lost its aim, and possibly its place in literature. It has ceased to give entertainment and has proffered nothing in exchange."

Strong stuff. And in the most thoroughgoing of his investigations into the appeal and the place of the detective story—an article called "The Novel Turns Tale"—Barzun has related his lifelong devotion to the genre to another preoccupation, what he sees as the exhaustion of the nineteenth-century concept of the novel. The bourgeois novel of character, of the Protestant conscience facing up to moral decisions in a massively detailed social context, of analytical studies of individuals and their dilemmas—this tradition had done all it could usefully do by the early twentieth century. It was played out, and if it did not die it could only repeat itself without the old exuberance or conviction. The only way the art of fiction could renew itself was by going back to older models, by seeking its inspiration, in fact, in the tale as opposed to the novel.

In the tale, closely allied to legend, fairy story, folk narratives and such like, the emphasis was fair and square on the storytelling elements, on seizing the reader's interest by incidents that might be thrilling, romantic, supernatural, totally fabulous. And this emphasis marks it off most definitely from the old realistic tradition of the novel, weighed down with character analyses and elaborate "atmosphere," in which the story often becomes no more than a regrettable necessity: "Oh dear yes," as Forster sighed, "the novel tells a story."

Thus Barzun stands out against the whole trend of recent writing on crime fiction which takes as its starting point the opening of Chandler's essay "The Simple Art of Murder," the patently untrue statement that "Fiction in any form has always intended to be realistic," and has thus viewed the crime story as limping fifty years late along the highway of realism, making its judgments and its critical distinctions on the basis of this shaky proposition.

One doesn't have to agree with all Barzun's contentions—with such a glorious tilter at windmills it would be patently impossible—to find this the most stimulating answer yet given to the problems presented by the detective story. I myself cannot see it as the reinvigorator of fiction, the successor to the novel proper: in fact the 'sixties and 'seventies seem to me to have been pretty good decades for the dear old bourgeois novel of the individual conscience, and there is something absurd about seeing a Dick Francis or an Alistair Maclean riding to the rescue of a tradition enfeebled to the point of a Drabble or a Lessing. Nor would I go along with another of Barzun's strong prejudices, his insistence on *detection* as the be-all and end-all of the detective story. This insistence is very strong in his *Catalogue of Crime*, and leads to some very odd judgments: how can one warm to a writer who despises Margery Allingham's Lugg, for example? In fact the detective formula has shown that it can embrace—in fact always has embraced—a lot more styles and approaches than Barzun would give it credit for, including the approach of the "hard-boiled" school.

But where I am sure he is right is in his insistence that we must cut off the modern detective story from the novel proper, put it in quite another category, one with its own traditions, conventions and demands, and thus develop a completely independent critical approach to it. I feel, in fact, that however we react to the novels of the American hard-boiled school, nothing but harm can be done by an attempt to see them as "realistic," or closer to the novel proper than other varieties of crime fiction. One hears so often these days the pronouncement that of course *detective* stories are trivial, escapist, utterly played out as a tradition, but that Chandler (or, more recently and incomprehensibly, Hammett) is another thing entirely. And the unwary general reader who acts on this cliché judgment and goes to Chandler or Hammett for the first time tends to come back with a puzzled frown on his face and an incipient shrug in his shoulder: what was all the fuss about? The same sort of misguided intellectual snobbery, seeking to make crime fiction respectable by making it what it is not, lies behind the judgment on Ross Macdonald, made by William Goldman in the *New York Times Book Review*, and which his English publishers use on the cover of paperback reprints: "One of the best American novelists now operating." The absurdity of such a pronouncement surely does not need underlining, and it nicely illustrates the harm we do to crime writers by using the novel proper as a way of placing them critically. If we insist that Chandler is a novelist, to be judged by putting him side by side with, say, Hemingway, Scott Fitzgerald or Sinclair Lewis, then one is forced to conclude that, however beautifully he may write, his plots are repetitive and intolerably clumsy, his characterization is superficial, his settings are monotonously sleazy and his "world view" a series of childish oversimplifications.

Nor will the much-touted "realism" of the hard-boiled school stand up to any very stringent examination. Books that concentrate their attention exclusively on gangsters, whores, and the corrupt superrich are every bit as partial in their scope and remote from the average reader's experience as books that concentrate on the genteel middle classes in the rural parts of Great Britain. If Christie has her stereotyped Anglo-Indian colonels and acidulated spinsters, how often do we meet in works of the California school the sexy middle-aged blonde with lust in her eyes and Martini on her breath? And if the average British policeman may blink at the goings-on of the investigators and the specimens of "detection" offered in the average Christie story, one wonders whether a real life private eye in the Los Angeles or San Francisco area will really feel a shock of recognition when he reads of the doings of a Philip Marlow or a Lew Archer.

No one would deny that the best of the hard-boiled school put up a better *appearance* of realism than a Christie or a Marsh, and hide more skillfully their reliance on popular fiction clichés. But it is only a skin-deep realism, as any comparison with a genuinely realistic novelist like Dreiser or Sinclair Lewis must show. Ross Macdonald's stories are plotted in a tight-knit, convoluted way, so that every incident and every person, however casually, met on Lew Archer's despondent quest through the Golden State turns out to be integral to the solution of the problem he is engaged on at the moment. He cannot pick up a hitchhiker or turn off into a motel without thereby acquiring a vital piece in the whole elaborate, linked-up puzzle which is a Macdonald plot. This is not a criticism—quite the reverse. Macdonald's plots are magnificently conceived, satisfyingly shaped, and splendidly entertaining. But they haven't got much to do with realism. And is California really so jampacked with adolescents who have witnessed a murder in their infancy?

If we stop trying to force Chandler, Macdonald and the rest (admittedly on their own insistence) into a mode that is totally uncongenial, that of the realistic novel, and try to see them as, like Christie, tellers of tales, then their quality becomes much more apparent: both embody personal myths about the destruction of innocence and the corrupting effects of great wealth and power in a series of highly wrought but exciting tales. They convey their vision by stereotyped characters and repetitive settings, which are given force by the obsessiveness of their private myth. What we read has only a marginal relation to the real world: it convinces us because it is a finely imagined fictional world, entire in itself, like the worlds of Tolkien or Peake, like the London of Dickens or the gloomy, hostile settings of the Gothic novelists. Or, of course, like the worlds of the English detective-story writers of the Golden Age. *The Big Sleep* looks much better in relation to *Clouds of Witness* or *The ABC Murders* than it does in relation to *The Great Gatsby*.

Because, in spite of differences of approach and ideology, the American and English crime writers are all writing thrillers, and all writing in the tradition of the tale rather than the novel. *Roger Ackroyd* is not a failed *Middlemarch*, and nothing but confusion results from trying to judge it by the same criteria. It is a work in a tradition which includes the Gothic novel, Elizabethan prose fiction, *Robinson Crusoe*, the tales of Boccaccio, *Dr. Jekyll and Mr. Hyde*, *The Picture of Dorian Gray* and a whole host of works which writers on "the novel" feel uneasy about, can't decide whether or not to include in their surveys, can't find categories within which to subsume them. Anyone who comes back to the Sherlock Holmes stories long after their childhood reading of them must surely get the vividest sense of their distinction—combined with an uneasy feeling that his habitual novel-reading has not given him the tools with which to analyze that distinction. The usual ones won't do: one can't deny the flatness of much of the writing, the four-squareness of the characterization, the conventionality of the moral code. And yet. . . .

It should surprise no one that the detective story should be so like the novel and yet should have its own rules and demands, which make a quite different yardstick necessary in judging it. One might cite an analogous case from another art. The opera singer who is hailed as a "great actress" would probably be tittered off stage if she took to acting with a provincial rep. Callas's way was that of a *singing-actress*, and her Violetta in *Traviata* would be totally unacceptable if it were transplanted into *La Dame aux Camellias*. Christie's procedures in *Roger Ackroyd* may look threadbare if we try to think of it as a novel, but they were right for a detective story.

The reasons why a Christie novel is so absorbing to so many hinge on her abilities as a storyteller and on the skill with which she mingles all or most of the ingredients of the main popular literary forms. Romantic interest, as we have seen, is no more than an incidental part of her books, and is treated very coolly: the reader is *not* encouraged to commit himself totally to the romantic experience offered. Excitement occupies a rather larger share of the interest, though her books can only nominally be included under the umbrella title "thrillers": in general they do not thrill. But she does manage the "big scene" in a way to involve or excite the reader, and she dots her books with stupendous revelations or bursts of action which keep the reader in a state of compulsive attention.

But the basis of Christie's success as a popular writer is the way she structures her books on a pattern of progressive mystification and progressive enlightenment. In the sections leading up to the murder the reader's interest is held by the gradual revelation of vital elements in the murder situation—though the revelation is frequently misleading, as we have seen, and thus mystification and enlightenment go hand in hand. They do too in the succeeding sections, in that she reveals information that has the effect of still further complicating the initial problem. But all these apparent complications are to be used in the final section when they fall together to form a total elucidation of everything that has hitherto baffled us. This structure of mystification and enlightenment is the basis of the excitement and the readability of a Christie story: not (as in a real thriller) a succession of incidents leading to a climax, but a progressive giving of information which eventually is to fall in place to form a total picture which illumines both the initial murder situation and the incidental mystifications of the actual killing. This total picture may have been there from the beginning, but obscured from the reader because the necessary information was fragmented or misplaced. The excitement of the book (and in this a Christie plot is little different from, say, a Ross Macdonald plot) lies in the ordering of this fragmentary information to form a recognizable and convincing whole.

Thus, she is not writing the sort of story which is character in action—where what happens must seem to spring inevitably from what the characters are, as in *Middlemarch* or *Portrait of a Lady*. She is writing a story where facts and incidents are of prime importance, and where characters must be tailored to suit them. She understood instinctively that the character interest of her stories had to be subordinate to her puzzles, must never be allowed to get out of hand. In this, as in so much else, she learned from Conan Doyle, whose characters flicker in brief, sufficient life on the printed page and then are forgotten. There is a fine character study inherent in what we are told about Professor Moriarty, but Conan Doyle doesn't bother to characterize him in the way that, say, Dickens would have done. Who could write more than a brief sentence on the various suspects in *The Hound of the Baskervilles*? They are sufficiently involving while we read, but they have no existence outside the puzzle which has called them into existence.

In fact, one could argue that, far from being her greatest deficiency, it is her characterization that gives Agatha Christie greater universality than all her rivals. If we go to her books looking for psychological depth, complex motivation, the exploration of unusual emotional states, we should at least be clear that we are looking for things that would not for a moment explain her mass popularity. And of course as a rule Agatha Christie provides none of these things. Almost all the well-known crime writers of her generation are "better" than she, judged by such criteria. If we are talking to a Christie enthusiast about, say, *Peril at End House* he may say, "Oh, that's the one that starts off with Poirot deciding that someone is trying to murder a girl, whereas in fact. . . ." In other words, it is the puzzle and its solution that he is likely to remember, the strategy Christie has used to deceive the reader. If the conversation goes beyond this and we start to talk about the other characters in the book, the chances are we neither of us will remember a single one. With Ngaio Marsh or Margery Allingham the reverse would apply. If we talk about *Opening Night* it is the theater milieu we will remember, and the young girl getting her first break on the West End stage. Or if we talk about *More Work for the Undertaker* we will remember the setting of Bloomsbury in decay and the family of eccentric individuals around whom the story revolves. But the chances are in both cases that we will have forgotten who did the murder.

And the vivid characterization and scene-setting of Allingham, wonderfully evocative though they are for readers of a certain British sociointellectual group, work against her as a popular writer. Bloomsbury, with its very special associations and particular atmosphere, means very little to the average lower-middle or working-class reader. By being so specific in her settings, by dwelling lovingly on the typical eccentricities of her characters, she loses universality.

Now the interesting thing about Agatha Christie is not only that she uses stereotypes for most or all of her suspects, but that her stereotypes are not even particularly vivid. There is a sort of general "feel" about her characters: anyone attending Anglican service in a rural community will recognise "Christie characters" in the sparse and shivering congregation around him. But they have very little individual coloring or specificity: one cannot distinguish between Major Burnaby, Major Horton, Major Porter and Major Palgrave. In fact, what she provides is a sort of basic outline, a bare minimum. She says, in effect: here is the outline shape of an Anglo-Indian, or a country squire, or a rural clergyman; fill in the details for yourself.

The same is true of her settings: there are many who depict the English village with more vividness and charm than Christie, but it is Christie who comes to people's minds when they think of the English village murder mystery. And it is the fact that she is not aiming at particularity, that her scene painting and characterization are marked by generality rather than vividness, that is her strength rather than her weakness, precisely this that gives her her universality. Her books are like a child's coloring-book, where the basic shape of the picture is provided, and the child fills in the details and decides on the colors himself.

I believe that the secret of Christie's worldwide appeal is that the Norwegian teenager and the middle-aged matron whom I mentioned in my first chapter, who know nothing of Anglo-Indian colonels or Church of England clergymen and who do not have them rendered vivid for them by the author, nevertheless manage to fill in the outline provided for them. And they do this with details drawn from *their own experience*. Thus, for example, the Italian lady relates the Anglo-Indian colonel to elderly Italian military men, veteran bores of the Albanian fiasco nostalgic for the age of Mussolini. The Norwegian girl can translate the Anglican clergyman into the subtly different Lutheran equivalent in communities she is familiar with. They can do this with Christie; they could not do it with Margery Allingham's Bloomsburyites because they are so particular and peculiar, and they are given such a special fictional life.

Thus, as I see it, Agatha Christie only seems to create a vision of England and English society; in fact she creates a broad, rather anonymous society on to which the reader can superimpose his own community, the human types that he himself is familiar with. Just as her characters gain universality *because* they have little psychological depth, *because* they are not vivid and particular, so also with the settings: because she cannot (or perhaps we should say, remembering the best of the Mary Westmacott novels, because she does not bother to) write well, Christie never creates any very evocative image of any particular place. One house or one village in her books is very like another. Even when the house is important (as for example in the posthumous *Sleeping Murder*) she avoids language with emotional overtones and gives it little or no architectural particularity. And because of this the reader supplies the details for himself, drawn from the houses or the communities he himself knows. My Norwegian teenager thinks she is reading about an English village, but what is really in her mind is an Anglo-Norwegian hybrid village, situated on a fjord somewhere near Torquay.

What I am trying to say about the reasons for Christie's universality is encapsulated in my own mind by an American paperback edition I own of *At Bertram's Hotel*. The cover depicts Miss Marple—a Miss Marple who is a well-preserved lady of a certain age, crowned with a magnificently coiffured head of blue-rinsed hair. But any outrage or amusement one might feel on the subject (and Agatha Christie would probably have felt the former) is tempered by the thought that if this is not how Christie imagined Miss Marple, it is certainly the way she is seen by the average American reader. He has recreated Miss Marple in a transatlantic mold.

The superb plotting and the adequate yet anonymous characterization go a long way to accounting for Agatha Christie's supremacy above all other twentieth-century detective-story writers. Something needs to be said too about her relation to the subject matter of her books—crime. I have suggested already that she took a conventional law-and-order approach, believed emphatically in punishment even unto hanging, and occasionally winked her steel-gray eyes at people who took the law into their own hands. But so far nothing has been said about the treatment of violence in her books, and this seems to me rather special. In *An Autobiography* she states unequivocally that when she began reading and writing detective stories she saw them as morality tales—"the hunting down of Evil and the triumph of Good"—and that for that reason she was shocked by the rather equivocal figure of Raffles (whom she seems to see, wrongly, as standing alone in the early detective story in his ambiguous relationship with the law):

> But Raffles was a light-hearted exception. No one could have dreamt then that there would come a time when crime books would be read for their love of violence, the taking of sadistic pleasure in brutality for its own sake. One would have thought the community would rise up in horror against such things; but now cruelty seems almost everyday bread and butter.

More than one reviewer at the time of publication (including Maurice Richardson in the *Observer*) suggested that Christie displays here a great lack of self-knowledge, and a naïve ignorance of why her books sell: after all, they were almost all about violent death, and they obviously appealed to the sadistic side of a public which delighted in tales of bloodshed and horror.

On the face of it Richardson and the others were undoubtedly right: with so many murders to her credit, many of them very bloody indeed, it must have seemed like gross hypocrisy, or at the very least self-deception, to complain about writers who take "sadistic pleasure in brutality for its own sake." And yet, on reflection, I think Agatha Christie was in the right, and many of the conventional explanations of the appeal of the English style of detective story wrong. That appeal is often described as that of "violence domesticated": people love the fact that these books bring the bloody events they usually only read about in the Sunday papers into the intimacy of their own sitting rooms—the appeal of "the body in the library," in fact.

But the more one reads of these books, and particularly the more one reads of Agatha Christie, the less such an explanation satisfies. Yes—no doubt the addict does like to have murder brought home to him, but not for any sadistic gloating over violence brought thrillingly close. What emotion does the average Christie reader feel when that body is discovered on the library door? Shock? Horror? Goose pimples around the nape of the neck? No. The primary reaction is surely along the lines of: "Right, here's the body. How is it lying? How long has it been dead? Are the windows open?" and so on. The violence in Christie arouses only the very mildest of frissons; the principal reaction is always intellectual and ratiocinative. None of her books aims at the sort of excitement Conan Doyle achieves in *The Hound of the Baskervilles* or *The Sign of Four:* due to the mode of presentation the violence does not shock or terrify. That Christie capitalizes on the public's interest in crime no one would deny, but it is not the sexual or sadistic interest aroused by, say, the deeds of a Jack the Ripper or her namesake Christie. It is the sort of interest that likes to speculate on exactly how Charles Bravo met his death, on whether conceivably Madeline Smith was innocent, or, for that matter, who it was who killed the Princes in the Tower. The interest in crime she appeals to is not an emotional and sensational one; it is a *curiosity*—the desire to examine the available facts and reason through from them to a convincing solution.

In fact, the sort of story Christie writes is the *only* popular form whose appeal is primarily to the mind, the faculty of reason, rather than to the emotions. Where the thriller invites emotional identification with the hero in his struggle against the forces of darkness, the most the detective form invites is a sort of participation in the continuing process of detection. The reader is a part of the investigative process, matching his wits against both criminal and detective. As John Ritchie says (in his excellent article "Agatha Christie's England 1918–1939"), her appeal "was essentially to the intellect, to the higher parts, divorced from the emotions and the sexual holts in contrast to the Bond stories of the 'fifties and 'sixties."

Of course, it may be objected that this appeal is on the lowest possible level: that her murders are as unlike any real murder that ever was committed as it is possible to be, and that the process of reasoning that takes place as a consequence is quite worthless, unrelated to any exercise of reason that might take place in everyday life, and therefore existing in a vacuum. But this is to ignore the fact that any popular form has to be granted its conventions: to enjoy James Bond we have to accept his world of pseudo-scientific, death-dealing gadgetry; to enjoy Daphne Du Maurier's *Frenchman's Creek* we have to suspend our skepticism about romantic French pirates; to enjoy a classic Western (alas, realism has invaded that genre too of late) we have to suspend our suspicions about the *real* nature of the men and women who pushed the frontier westward.

Grant the conventions of the detective story, which are no more absurd than those governing any other popular genre, and one ought to respect it as appealing primarily to a human instinct to reason through, to form a total picture from fragmented pieces, to use the brain to bring order from chaos and light from darkness. In fact, Agatha Christie—far from deceiving herself about the place of violence in her books—deserves great credit for shunning the cheaper sorts of titillation and, especially in her classic phase, for conceiving a series of superb puzzles, thought through with great intellectual rigor and put before the reader with scrupulous fairness. Much of the average reader's affection for Christie (a feeling she certainly arouses, even though, with her hatred and distrust of publicity, she did nothing extra-literary to stimulate it) springs from the fact that, within the limitations of this particular popular form, she appealed to his mind, and treated it with respect.

And this unique appeal to the mind is why—however often the funeral service is read over it—the classic whodunnit will never die. Even now, as was suggested earlier, it probably has more *readers* than any other popular form. As far as younger writers are concerned it may well be that it was killed not by any inherent artificiality, not because it ran out of variations, but by its acquired snobbery, which the new generation found repulsive and irrelevant to the world they wanted to depict. When they realize that the formula is infinitely adaptable, can flourish in any setting, with characters of any class or race, can make a genuine comment on the social and moral condition of the world today, then the whodunnit may return in force—perhaps has already begun to do so. It is worth noting that some of the more recent practitioners of the California school, for example, the much-praised Brown Meggs, superimpose a relentlessly realistic style of characterization and setting on to distinctly Christiean tricks of plotting. He is not the only one to find that the formula is infinitely adaptable, as well as being, for most readers, marvelously entertaining.

It was Christie's great strength that she never forgot that she was an entertainer, never pretended to be anything other than a popular writer. Jacques Barzun's complaint that with its new realism, psychological and social, the detective story has "ceased to give entertainment" may be an exaggeration, but it contains the seeds of truth, and constitutes a terrible warning. Christie was, by his definition, a teller of tales, and content to remain so. It was distrusting the value of tales that led Dorothy L. Sayers from being a writer of lively detective stories to being a writer of mediocre middle-brow novels. However much Lord Peter may irritate, however much the racial and social attitudes may repel, one cannot deny that *Clouds of Witness* and *The Unpleas-antness at the Bellona Club* are highly entertaining stories, with some wonderfully tricky detection. Who in their senses would exchange them for the longueurs of *Have His Carcase* or *Gaudy Night*? And because of her prestige and her evangelist instincts Sayers spread the disease well beyong her own work: several Allingham books of the late 'thirties (for example, *The Fashion in Shrouds*) became allusive and pretentious precisely by aiming to be that most shiver-making thing "a respectable form of literature." Josephine Tey also squirmed with the detective formula (had she not written dull historical plays?) and began producing entertaining novelettes with a mildly detective flavor. From all such ambitions Agatha Christie was blessedly free. She always knew what she was: "one is a tradesman—a tradesman in a good honest trade."

And if she had no desire to elevate her "trade" into a "profession" by writing anything that could be confused with a "real novel," still less was she bitten by the fine-writing bug. Her own estimate of her capacities in that direction has been quoted, and it is modest but not unfair. She could write competently—she certainly might without detriment have taken a little more care. But her good sense saved her from the sort of ambitions nourished by her foremost rival: just as Sayers's idea of making the detective story intellectually respectable was to have her characters fling around quotations as if they were Ping-Pong balls, so her idea of literary style was a pretentious and convoluted mishmash, like George Eliot in gumboots. The main characteristic of Agatha Christie's writing is that one does not notice it. And that, perhaps, is about the highest praise one could give to a writer of popular literature.

In fact, all the common grounds of criticism and ridicule used against Agatha Christie work with a boomerang effect when we realize that she was essentially, and aimed to be, a popular writer, a good teller of tales. Her drab style is admirably suited to such an aim. We do not go to popular literature for fine writing, we go to it for relief from fine writing. Our main requirement is that the author gets on with the story and doesn't allow anything to interfere with the narrative flow, and this she invariably does. Similarly with characterization and setting, as we have seen: in the tale they must be subordinate to the incidents; they must support them but not obtrude themselves into too independent an existence. By never luxuriating in her exotic settings, or sentimentalizing her English ones; by never letting any one character loom too large (if he does, like Mrs. Boynton, we can be sure he will soon be removed) or monopolize interest by too great a psychological complexity, she places the interest fair and square where in popular literature it belongs—in the narration of events.

All her supposed weaknesses are thus part of her strength as a popular writer. And the beauty of that narrative which she places at the forefront of the interest, and plans so meticulously, is that, like a bud opening into flower, we have a sense of initial mystery and concealment which gradually unfolds to reveal a design of patterned intricacy and beauty. And by this progression from meaningful mystery to enlightenment, the pattern of all her best books, she mirrors every reader's experience of life around him—the deceiving surfaces of it, the façades other people put up before their neighbor's inquiring gaze, which gradually come down and give way to a deeper knowledge of the passions that drive them. Her books are the literary equivalent of that most universal human curiosity, the desire to penetrate the secrets of our fellow humans' lives.

What will be the fate of her books in the next fifty, the next hundred years is anybody's guess. One thing we can be sure of: those who regard the Sherlock Holmes societies and reenactments of the famous fatality at the Reichenbach Falls as a species of the higher lunacy we can well do without can surely rest assured that no similar cult will embrace Poirot, Hastings, George and Miss Lemon. They lack the recognizable humanity of Holmes and Watson, and the densely imagined physical environment as well. They do not have sufficient independence as creations to affect people's imaginations in that way. And could one, today, find a St. Mary Mead to build a cult around?

But that the English detective stories of the Golden Age can take hold of people's imaginations in a quite other way is evidenced by the multitude of recent parodies I mentioned earlier. Joe Orton and his friend Kenneth Halliwell went to jail for defacing, among other books, a Peter Wimsey novel with a cod blurb promising all sorts of indecent surprises in the course of the noble lord's investigations. But when he came to write *Loot* Orton sent up the conventions of the classical detective story in a way that was not only hilarious, but also affectionate. The stuff of the whodunnit became the material for many un-Christiean reflections on the nature of British law and justice, but it also was transformed into fantastical farce of a truly Wildean delicacy and wit. I doubt whether this could have happened if the material Orton was parodying did not have in itself a literary vitality of some sort, and did not genuinely answer some human craving.

One is reminded of the fashion in the early nineteenth century for writing sendups of the popular "Gothic" novels: parodies of one kind or another were written by Peacock, Byron, Jane Austen, and others, and most of these parodies suggest that the ridicule was inspired by affection rather than contempt. The strength of *Northanger Abbey* lies not only in the fact that it hilariously parodies a form that was ripe for ridicule; as many critics have pointed out, it is effective because Jane Austen acknowledges the force of the Gothic novel's appeal to one side of herself—an emotional, sensation-craving side that she usually found it necessary to suppress in her writing. The same is true of Orton and the other modern parodists of the detective story: while they ridicule its artificiality and snobbery, they acknowledge the appeal it makes to sides of their nature which it is unfashionable to indulge—a love of order, certainty, rationality.

And it may be that, just as—in spite of the ridicule of the intellectuals of the time—the Gothic novel still maintains a toe-hold in English literature, continues to be read by devotees and even recreated by a Daphne du Maurier, so perhaps the detective story of the classic British type will maintain a similar fringe literary existence, never quite accepted or respectable yet not entirely cast out on to the garbage heaps of forgotten literary fashion—a Duchess of Windsor sort of existence, never quite in and never quite out.

Certain it is that Agatha Christie's durability is already astonishing, and shows no sign of waning. Ian Fleming has been dead only fifteen years, but already one can see signs that Bond has peaked and is in decline, needing badly the hormone injections of those bad films. Roger Ackroyd was murdered more than fifty years ago, yet there are still as many people as ever who care who killed him. The irritation one felt at the garrulity and the slackened grip of those last Christie novels cannot alter the fact that Christmas has not felt the same these last few years without her offering. Already the signs are that she will not suffer seriously from the slump in reputation that most writers experience after their death. So already we are beginning to get the idea that as well as spanning age, intelligence and class barriers she will jump the gap that separates her era from succeeding ones.

Why? She created a timeless, changeless world, peopled by cardboard characters who somehow manage to maintain our interest in that dazzling conjuring trick that is to be performed on page 190. She nourished our instinctive hopes that in the end right and truth will triumph over the evil and the obscure. And she brought murder into the home, where it belonged, seeing the murderous glint in the eye of the self-effacing bank clerk, the homicidal madness in the flutterings of the genteel lady companion. Chandler saw evil in the social organisms of which we are part; Christie saw it in our wives, our friends, the quiet circle of which we are a part. And perhaps thereby she made us sense it in ourselves.

CHARLES OSBORNE

Appearance and Disappearance

The Mysterious Affair at Styles (1920)

It was while she was married to Archie Christie that Agatha Christie, *neé* Miller, wrote and published her first novel, *The Mysterious Affair at Styles*. That marriage lasted for less than fourteen years, ending in divorce at about the time of publication of her ninth book, *The Mystery of the Blue Train*, but her career as a writer of crime fiction continued for a further half-century and a further eighty-five titles (excluding the plays). Having become known to a vast reading public as Agatha Christie, the author continued to use that name for professional purposes throughout the rest of her life, although privately she became Mrs Max Mallowan soon after her divorce from Christie.

Agatha Miller was born in the elegant, sedate seaside resort of Torquay, Devonshire, on the south coast of England, on 15 September 1890, at Ashfield, the home of her parents, Frederick and Clarissa Miller. Frederick Alvah Miller was a well-to-do young American who lived as much in England, where he had relatives, as in America, on an income derived from the family business. After he married Clarissa Margaret Beochmer (his step-mother's niece) he and his wife planned to live in America. However, they first spent some time in Torquay, at the height of the winter season, and Mr

From *The Life and Crimes of Agatha Christie* by Charles Osborne. © 1982 by Holt, Rinehart and Winston.

Miller, who loved the sea, became enchanted with the town, its attractive bay and the dramatic south Devon coast. The Millers' first child, Marjorie (Madge) was born in Torquay, shortly after which the family left for America where they expected to make their permanent home. It was while they were staying with Frederick Miller's grandparents in New England that their second child, Louis (Monty), was born.

The Millers returned to England for a visit, but Mr Miller was almost immediately recalled to New York by business concerns, and therefore suggested to his wife that she should take the children and rent a furnished house in Torquay until his return. What Clara Miller did, instead, was to buy a house in Torquay from a Quaker family called Brown. Extremely placid by temperament, Mr Miller, though surprised, did not remonstrate. The house could, after all, be sold again in a year's time. The Millers and their two children moved into the house, Ashfield, and Mr Miller found life in Torquay so agreeable that in due course he decided that they may as well settle there. Ashfield, a large and comfortable villa with green lawns, a garden of about two acres, and great beech trees, made a splendid home for Mrs Miller and the children even though it was not in the most fashionable part of Torquay but in Barton Road, in the older, upper-middleclass district of Tor Mohun.

When a third child was born to the Millers, a good eight years after the second, she was christened Agatha May Clarissa. The second and third were family names, but 'Agatha' appears to have been suggested by a friend of Mrs Miller on the way to the christening. A chubby redhead, Agatha turned out to be a quiet, imaginative child who played a great deal on her own or with her elderly nannie, 'Nursy', since her brother and sister were away at school for much of the time and were, in any case, so much older than she. Agatha did not go to school but taught herself to read, and learned something of elementary mathematics from her father. Her formal education did not begin until, at the age of sixteen, she was sent to a finishing school in Paris. Her father had died when she was eleven, and the family income had dwindled. Mrs Miller considered selling Ashfield but was prevailed upon by her two elder children merely to reduce the number of servants and make certain other economies.

The Millers were still able to live comfortably. With Madge married and living in New York, and Monty serving with the army in India, Mrs Miller decided shortly after Agatha's return from finishing school in Paris that she would let Ashfield furnished for three months and take her teenage daughter off to Egypt. Her own health had not been good, but three months with Agatha in and around Cairo, sight-seeing, going to dances and parties and on excursions to the sites of antiquity, seemed to improve her condition and certainly helped Agatha to overcome her childhood and adolescent *gaucherie*. The attractive young lady even received several proposals of marriage from officers serving in the British Army in Egypt, but took none of them seriously. She was still very young, and she was also now her mother's only comfort and companion. When they returned to Torquay, Agatha continued to live at home with her mother, though she also led an active social life with friends of her own age.

Agatha had already begun to write. During her childhood, when she was lying in bed recovering from influenza, her mother had suggested that, instead of telling stories which she enjoyed doing, she should write one of them down. Soon Agatha had produced a number of stories, and began to write poems as well. It was as a poet that she made her first appearance in print, at the age of eleven, with a poem about the new electric trams which she had seen when visiting her grandmother at Ealing, a suburb of London. The poem, which was printed in the local Ealing newspaper, began: 'When first the electric trams did run/In all their scarlet glory,/ 'Twas well, but ere the day was done,/It was another story.'

Her poems improved, and by the time she was in her late teens Agatha had won a few prizes with them, usually of a guinea or so offered by the Poetry Society, and had had several poems published in *The Poetry Review*. She had also written a number of stories which, as she said later, usually revealed the influence of whomever she had been reading the previous week, as often as not D. H. Lawrence. Under various pseudonyms, among them Mack Miller and Nathanael Miller (her grandfather's name), she would send her stories off to magazines and they would invariably come back to her accompanied by a printed rejection slip. She even attempted a novel, which she called *Snow Upon the Desert*, and at the suggestion of her mother sent it off to Eden Phillpotts, the author of popular novels of Devon rural life in the tradition of Thomas Hardy. (In the twenties and thirties, Phillpotts was to write murder mysteries, both under his own name and as Harrington Hext.)

Phillpotts, who was a neighbour of the Millers and a friend of the family, gave generously of his time and advice. Though he was critical of *Snow Upon the Desert*, and advised its author to cut out the moralizing of which he considered she was much too fond, he thought Agatha had a 'great feeling for dialogue', and introduced her to his literary agent, Hughes Massie. Agatha went to London and was interviewed by Mr Massie, a large, swarthy man who, she said, terrified her. Massie read her novel, and advised her to put it aside and begin another. Instead, she returned to writing her poems and stories

Agatha was now in her early twenties and fending off young men who wished to marry her. After what she referred to as two near escapes, she became engaged in 1912 to Reggie Lucy, a Major in the Gunners, but while

Lucy was serving with his regiment in Hong Kong, she fell in love with a handsome young Lieutenant in the Royal Field Artillery, whom she had met at a house party in Chudleigh, not far from Torquay. He was Lieutenant Archibald Christie, the son of a Judge in the Indian Civil Service. They danced together several times at their first meeting, and a few days later Christie arrived on his motorcycle at Ashfield and was allowed by Mrs Miller to stay to supper. Within days, he and Agatha had become engaged, and Agatha eventually plucked up the courage to write to Reggie Lucy in Hongkong ending their engagement.

It was eighteen months later that Agatha Miller married Archie Christie, now a Captain in the Royal Flying Corps. The wedding took place on Christmas Eve, 1914. During the period of their engagement, the Miller family income had been further depleted by the liquidation of a firm in New York, and Britain had declared war on Germany. Captain Christie went off to war two days after the wedding, while his bride went to work at the Torbay Hospital in Torquay, nursing the first casualties who were being brought back from the Front. After two years of nursing, and a number of reunions with Archie when he came home on leave, Agatha transferred to the hospital's dispensary, where she acquired the accurate knowledge of poisons which was later to prove so useful to her.

Years earlier, Agatha and her sister Madge had one day been discussing a murder mystery they were reading, and Agatha had mentioned, idly, that she would like to try her hand at a detective story. Madge was of the opinion that Agatha would find this too difficult a task, an opinion which Agatha remembered in 1916, while working in the hospital dispensary at Torquay. She decided to devote her occasional slack periods at the dispensary to the composition of a detective novel, in the hope of proving her sister wrong.

Her first problem, as Agatha Christie revealed many years later in her autobiography, was to decide what kind of detective story she would write. Since she was surrounded by poisons, it was natural that death by poisoning should be the method she selected. She settled on one particular fact or *donné* which seemed to her to have possibilities, toyed with the idea for a time, and finally decided upon it. Next she turned to the *dramatis personae*. Who should be poisoned? Who would be the poisoner? When? Where? How? Why? It would, she decided, have to be 'very much of an *intime* murder', because of the method chosen. It would have to be all in the family, so to speak.

And, of course, there would have to be a detective to unravel the mystery and unmask the evil-doer. An avid reader of the Sherlock Holmes stories of Sir Arthur Conan Doyle, Agatha pondered upon the personality and methods of Holmes and his relationship with Dr Watson, his friend and the chronicler of his cases. Her detective, she decided, would have to be as different in personality from Sherlock Holmes as possible. However, the device of the friend and helper, the Dr Watson–figure whose obtuseness sets off the brilliant deductive powers of the great detective, was too useful to discard. Her detective would, therefore, have such a figure in attendance, and he could be the narrator of the story.

The budding crime writer now had an idea for the actual crime, and a detective and his aide. But who were the other characters to be? Who was to be murdered? Husbands frequently murdered their wives, of course, but perhaps it would be better to opt for a more unusual kind of murder and for a very unusual motive. But then the whole point of a really good murder mystery was that the criminal should be someone obvious, whose obviousness was not apparent until pointed out in the last chapter by the brilliant detective. At this point in her reasoning, Agatha Christie confessed later, she became confused and went away to make up a couple of extra bottles of hypochlorous lotion, so that she would have more free time the following day to give further consideration to her crime project.

Over the next few days, her plot began to develop in some detail, though in a somewhat unorthodox manner. Having first decided what she wanted her murderer to look like, Agatha next began to search around among her acquaintances for someone who fitted the description, in order to study his physical characteristics. She soon realized, however, that it was pointless to attempt to base a fictional character upon a real person's characteristics. Later, with experience, she would find ways of doing this to some extent, but for the present she was in need of a starting-off point. She found it when, sitting in a tram, she saw exactly what she wanted: 'a man with a black beard, sitting next to an elderly lady who was chattering like a magpie.' As she did not know these people, her imagination was unfettered; she could invent characters for them, and place them in situations of her own invention.

She continued to give consideration to the question of the detective. It was important that he should not be simply an imitation Sherlock Holmes. What other models were there? Arsène Lupin? The young journalist Rouletabille in *The Mystery of the Yellow Room?* Perhaps the detective could be a scientist. Or a schoolboy? A schoolboy would be too difficult, and Agatha was not acquainted with any scientists. Then she remembered the colony of Belgian war refugees who were living in the parish of Tor, in Torquay. Might not one of them be a Belgian police officer? A retired Belgian police officer, not too young:

> I allowed him slowly to grow into his part. He should have
> been an inspector, so that he would have a certain knowledge
> of crime. He would be meticulous, very tidy, I thought to

myself, as I cleared away a good many untidy odds and ends
in my own bedroom. A tidy little man. I could see him as a
tidy little man, always arranging things, liking things in pairs,
liking things square instead of round. And he should be very
brainy—he should have little grey cells of the mind—that was
a good phrase: I must remember that—yes, he would have
little grey cells. He would have rather a grand name—one of
those names that Sherlock Holmes and his family had. Who
was it his brother had been? Mycroft Holmes.

Since he was to be a little man, it seemed an amusing idea to name the
retired detective Hercules, the hero of Greek myth. Where did 'Poirot' come
from? Did Agatha Christie think of her little detective as also being pear
(*poire*)-shaped? Later, she was unable to remember. But she liked the sound
of 'Hercule Poirot', and enthusiastically set to work on the other characters
and on the plot, inventing situations, revelations and false clues during her
leisure time at the dispensary and at home. Eventually, she began to write her
novel, using a battered old typewriter that had belonged to her sister. Her
method was to produce a first draft of each chapter in longhand and then
revise the chapter as she typed it.

About halfway through, Agatha began to find herself in difficulties
with her complicated plot, at which point her mother suggested that, if she
was ever going to bring her novel to a successful conclusion, she should
take the typescript away with her on her holiday from the hospital, and
work at it with nothing else to distract her. And so, in the summer of 1916,
Mrs Archibald Christie took herself off to beautiful, grey, remote Dartmoor, quite near Torquay in distance, but a world away in atmosphere with
its rugged moorland, giant granite tors on craggy hills, ancient stone
circles, and prehistoric remains.

Much of the 365 square miles of Dartmoor is bleak country, with
treacherous bogs. But a few hundred yards from the summit of Hay Tor, the
Moorland Hotel is situated, partially hidden by trees, with views over the
moor and across South Devon to the sea, and it was there that Agatha
Christie lived for two weeks while she finished writing the murder mystery
which she had decided to call *The Mysterious Affair at Styles*. The hotel is still
there, though it has been closed since fire destroyed some of its rooms in
March, 1970. Years later, Agatha Christie described her two weeks' stay at
the Moorland Hotel in 1916:

It was a large, dreary hotel with plenty of rooms. There were
few people staying there. I don't think I spoke to any of

them—it would have taken my mind away from what I was doing. I used to write laboriously all morning till my hand ached. Then I would have lunch, reading a book. Afterwards I would go out for a good walk on the moor, perhaps for a couple of hours. I think I learned to love the moor in those days. I loved the tors and the heather and all the wild part of it away from the roads. Everybody who went there—and of course there were not many in wartime—would be clustering around Hay Tor itself, but I left Hay Tor severely alone and struck out on my own across country. As I walked, I muttered to myself, enacting the chapter that I was next going to write; speaking as John to Mary, and as Mary to John; as Evelyn to her employer, and so on. I became quite excited by this. I would come home, have dinner, fall into bed and sleep for about twelve hours. Then I would get up and write passionately again all morning.

When Archie Christie came home on leave, he read his wife's novel and enjoyed it. A friend of his in the Air Force was a director of another publishing house, Methuen's, and Archie suggested that if her novel was returned again to Agatha, he would provide her with a letter from his friend which she could enclose with the typescript and send off to Methuen's. This plan was duly followed but, although Methuen's sat on the typescript for about six months, perhaps to prove to Archie's friend that they were giving it their most earnest consideration, they eventually concluded that it was not quite suitable for them, and returned it to its author.

The Mysterious Affair at Styles was submitted to a fourth publisher, again without success, after which Agatha decided to try The Bodley Head, having noticed that they had recently published one or two detective novels. She packed the manuscript off to them, heard nothing, and forgot all about it.

Towards the end of the war, Archie Christie, now a Colonel, was posted to the Air Ministry in London, so Agatha was able to leave Torquay and live at last with her husband. They took a small flat in St John's Wood, at 5 Northwick Terrace, which was really no more than two rooms on the second floor of a house (now demolished), and Agatha started a course of book-keeping and shorthand to occupy her days. The war came to an end, and a few months later, in 1919 Mrs Christie gave birth to a daughter, Rosalind, at Ashfield, the family home in Torquay.

The Christies now needed a larger London flat, and in due course found what they were looking for on the fourth floor of Addison Mansions (Flat 96), a huge double apartment block behind Olympia in Earl's Court.

Archie was demobilized, and went to work for a firm in the City. It was towards the end of 1919, nearly two years after she had sent the typescript of *The Mysterious Affair at Styles* to The Bodley Head, that Agatha Christie received a letter from John Lane, the Managing Director of the publishing house, asking her to call and see him. When they met, John Lane explained that several people had read her novel and thought it showed promise. However, the dénouement, which she had written as a courtroom scene, did not ring true. If Mrs Christie would rewrite that chapter, in a different setting, and make some other minor changes, The Bodley Head would be willing to publish her book.

After explaining what a risk he was taking by offering to publish a new and unknown writer, and how little money he was likely to make with her novel, John Lane produced a contract from the drawer of his desk, and an excited young author who had given up hope of ever having anything published, other than the occasional story or poem, immediately signed it. She was to receive a small royalty, but only after the first 2,000 copies had been sold. All subsidiary rights, such as serialization and film rights, would be shared fifty-fifty between author and publisher, and there was a clause binding the author to offer The Bodley Head her next five novels, at an only slightly increased royalty rate. A jubilant Agatha rushed home to inform her husband of her good fortune, and that evening they celebrated at the Hammersmith Palais de Danse.

When *The Mysterious Affair at Styles* was published in 1920, it sold nearly 2,000 copies. The £25 which Agatha Christie earned from her first book came, not from royalties, for there were none due to her under the terms of a distinctly unfair contract, but from a half share of the serial rights which had been sold for £50 to *The Weekly Times*. Taking the view that £25 was not a very satisfactory return for all the time and energy she had expended upon the writing of her novel, Agatha did not envisage ever attempting to write another. At least, this is what she was to claim, years later, in her autobiography. She had been dared by her sister to write a detective story, she had done so, and she had got it published. There, as far as she was concerned, the matter ended. She would probably write stories from time to time, but she had no intention of turning herself into a professional writer. To her, writing was fun.

In this, as in one or two other matters, Agatha Christie's *An Autobiography* is less than completely reliable. Writing it over a number of years between 1950 and 1965, she did not always remember with accuracy events which had taken place thirty or forty years earlier. In fact, in a letter to Basil Willett of The Bodley Head, written in the autumn of 1920, she inquired about the publication date of *The Mysterious Affair at Styles*, adding that she was beginning to wonder if it was ever going to appear, as she had already nearly finished a second novel, *The Secret Adversary*. She also wanted to know what the cover of *The Mysterious Affair at Styles* would look like. After she had seen the cover design, she agreed that it would do as it was 'quite artistic and mysterious'. She also asked that a dedication, 'To my mother', should appear at the beginning of the book.

Most of the qualities which were to make Agatha Christie the most popular crime writer there has ever been were already on display in *The Mysterious Affair at Styles*, and it is astonishing that several publishers turned the novel down before it was accepted by The Bodley Head. Characterization is no more detailed than Agatha Christie needed it to be for her purpose, the setting is an English country house in or near a small village, there is a proliferation of clues which are there for the reader to discover, if he is not dazzled by the author's sleight of hand, and the method used by the murderer is poisoning.

The young Agatha Christie had learned a great deal about poisons through her work at the hospital dispensary in Torquay, and she was to put her knowledge to good use in several of her murder mysteries. Among the many favourable reviews her excellent first novel received, Agatha was especially proud of that in the *Pharmaceutical Journal* which praised 'this detective story for dealing with poisons in a knowledgeable way, and not with the nonsense about untraceable substances that so often happens. Miss Agatha Christie knows her job.'

The 'Styles' of the title is Styles Court, a country house in Essex, a mile outside the village of Styles St. Mary. In later novels, Mrs Christie tended not to specify the county, and even in this first novel she avoids using real names of towns. Characters may take the train up to London from the country, but if they have to visit a nearby country town it will not be identified as Chelmsford or Colchester, but will be given a fictitious name. The fictitious village of Styles St. Mary is, for instance, seven miles away from the fictitious town of Tadminster, where one of the characters works in the dispensary of the Red Cross Hospital.

The Mysterious Affair at Styles, though not published until 1920, had been written during the First World War, and was set in the summer of 1916. Its narrator, Captain Hastings, is a young officer who has been invalided home from the Front and who, after spending some months 'in a rather depressing Convalescent Home', is still on sick leave when he runs into someone he had known as a boy: the forty-five-year-old John Cavendish who is 'a good fifteen years' Hastings' senior. Hastings, then, is about thirty. Reading *The Mysterious Affair at Styles* now, the reader interests himself more in Captain Hastings' personal details than Agatha Christie's readers would have done in 1920, for they were not to know that Mrs Christie would go on to write scores of crime novels over the years and that Hastings would figure in eight of them (and in numerous short stories) as the associate of her detective, Hercule Poirot.

John Cavendish invites the convalescent Hastings to spend his leave in Essex at Styles Court. Cavendish's stepmother, whom Hastings remembered as a handsome, middle-aged woman, is now an autocratic grande dame of seventy or more. After several years of widowhood, she has recently married Alfred Inglethorp, who is about twenty years younger than she, and 'an absolute bounder' in the opinion of John Cavendish because he has 'a great black beard, and wears patent leather boots in all weathers'. Clearly, Alfred Inglethorp is a fortune-hunter, for Mrs Inglethorp has a sizeable fortune to dispose of. When she is found murdered, he is the chief and favourite suspect.

The other inhabitants of Styles Court include John Cavendish's wife Mary, his younger brother Lawrence, a girl called Cynthia who is a protégé of Mrs Inglethorp and who works in the dispensary of the nearby hospital, and Evelyn Howard, a forty-year-old woman who has been the old lady's companion, factotum and general assistant. There is also a tall, bearded and somewhat mysterious foreigner, a Dr Bauerstein, who is staying in the village, recuperating after a nervous breakdown. He is said to be one of the greatest living experts on poisons.

When Mrs Inglethorp's death, at first thought to be due to a heart attack, is found to have been caused by strychnine poisoning, suspicion falls not only upon her husband but, in turn, on most of her nearest and dearest. The local police are called in, but Hastings has encountered in the village an old friend of his, Hercule Poirot, a famous detective now retired, and it is Hastings who persuades his friend John Cavendish to allow Poirot as well to investigate the crime.

Before the First World War, young Hastings had worked for Lloyd's of London. (Not until *The ABC Murders* in 1935 shall we learn Hastings' first name to be Arthur, for Agatha Christie's men habitually address each other in what used to be the approved English upper-middleclass fashion, by their surnames.) It was while he was working for Lloyd's that Hastings had first met Poirot, in Belgium. Poirot had already retired from the Belgian Police Force, after a long career as its most illustrious detective, and had set himself up in private practice as an investigator. Hastings is surprised and delighted to meet him again unexpectedly in the village of Styles St Mary where Poirot, together with a number of other Belgian refugees, is living. Poirot accepts with alacrity the commission to find Mrs Inglethorp's murderer, for, as he explains to Hastings, 'she had kindly extended hospitality to seven of my countrypeople who, alas, are refugees from their native land.' 'We Belgians,' he adds, 'will always remember her with gratitude.'

Poirot, on his first appearance, is described in some detail:

> He was hardly more than five feet, four inches, but carried
> himself with great dignity. His head was exactly the shape of
> an egg, and he always perched it a little on one side. His
> moustache was very stiff and military. The neatness of his
> attire was almost incredible; I believe a speck of dust would
> have caused him more pain than a bullet wound.

Later, we shall discover that Poirot is not only fanatically neat but is also
obsessed with symmetry. He is forever rearranging the objects he encoun-
ters, putting them into straight rows. He probably wished that eggs were
square: he certainly, on one occasion, deplored the fact that hens lay eggs of
different sizes ('What symmetry can there be on the breakfast table?'). It is
odd, therefore, that he should habitually carry his head tilted a little to one
side. He cannot have been aware that he did so.

Poirot will acquire other personality traits in later books, or at least we
shall learn more about him, but already apparent in *Styles* are his genuine
affection for Hastings of whose perspicacity he has a justifiably low opinion,
his endearing vanity, his odd misuse of the English language and still odder
occasional misuse of his native tongue, French (for, despite her Paris
finishing school, Mrs Christie's French was to remain obstinately unid-
iomatic). Incidentally, when he sees his old friend for the first time in several
years, Hastings notices that Poirot now limps badly. But the limp is never
referred to again: we must assume that it was a temporary disability from
which Poirot soon recovered. Indeed, when he inspects Mrs Inglethorp's
room at Styles Court, Poirot, we are told, 'darted from one object to the
other with the agility of a grasshopper.'

Just as 'Elementary, my dear Watson', (which is not a direct quotation
from any story by Sir Arthur Conan Doyle) is the phrase you most associate
with Sherlock Holmes, so a habit of constantly referring to 'the little grey cells'
of the brain is something closely associated with Hercule Poirot. But, though
he is continually having 'little ideas', and recommending order and method to
Hastings, Poirot mentions the 'little grey cells' for the first time only towards
the end of *Styles*. He makes a point, however, of informing Hastings (and the
reader of the book) well before the dénouement that 'I am not keeping back
facts. Every fact that I know is in your possession. You can draw your own
deductions from them.' Hastings, however, never wins a battle of wits with
Hercule Poirot, and it is a reasonable assumption that even the most assiduous
reader of Agatha Christie will do so only rarely.

Agatha Christie was conscious of the necessity to make Poirot very
different from the most famous fictional detective of his day, Sherlock

Holmes. After all, Conan Doyle's Sherlock Holmes adventures were still appearing. *The Valley of Fear* was published in 1915, *His Last Bow* in 1917, and *The Casebook of Sherlock Holmes* in 1927. But it is only physically that Poirot differs greatly from Holmes. The two detectives share a number of qualities, among which vanity is by no means the least noticeable. Still, if Poirot owes something to Conan Doyle and Sherlock Holmes, does he not also owe something to another crime novelist? Mrs Belloc Lowndes, sister of Hilaire Belloc, and writer of a number of historical and mystery novels and stories, was the creator of a detective who, like Poirot, was foreign, retired (in his case, from the Paris Sûreté), and incredibly vain. His name was Hercules Popeau. Agatha Christie must certainly have been aware of him when she began to write her first Hercule Poirot novel, and indeed throughout the nineteen-twenties and -thirties when stories by Mrs Belloc Lowndes, featuring Popeau, appeared in the same anthologies as stories of Hercule Poirot's exploits. In the mid-thirties, Mrs Belloc Lowndes published a Popeau story, 'A Labour of Hercules', which did not deter Mrs Christie in the mid-forties from calling a collection of Poirot stories *The Labours of Hercules.*

Devoted Christieans, who delight in assembling the 'facts' about Poirot in the same manner that Conan Doyle's more fanatical admirers tend to research the great Sherlock Holmes, have somehow convinced themselves that Poirot retired from the Belgian Police Force in 1904, and that this fact is revealed in *The Mysterious Affair at Styles*. It is not. We are told that Poirot 'had been in his time one of the most celebrated members of the Belgian Police.' When, late in the story, Inspector James Japp of Scotland Yard puts in an appearance (he is the Christiean equivalent of Sherlock Holmes's sparring partner, Inspector Lestrade), he greets Poirot and then, turning to a colleague, says: 'You've heard me speak of Mr Poirot? It was in 1904 he and I worked together—the Abercrombie forgery case—you remember, he was run down in Brussels. Ah, those were great days, moosier. Then do you remember "Baron" Altara? There was a pretty rogue for you! He eluded the clutches of half the police in Europe. But we nailed him in Antwerp—thanks to Mr Poirot here.'

Poirot, then, was active in his post in 1904, and the 'Baron' Altara affair may well have occurred after 1904. It is possible that Poirot's retirement did not take place until 1914, in which case he could have been as young as sixty-seven at the time of the Styles murder in 1916. (In *Murder on the Links*, published three years after *Styles*, we learn that Poirot was still active in Ostend in 1909.) Agatha Christie later declared that, if she had realized how long she was going to be saddled with Poirot, she would have made him a much younger man on his first appearance. It is fortunate that fictional chronology can be flexible, for otherwise Poirot would have been at least one hundred and twenty years of age when he came to solve his final case in 1974, after having featured in thirty-three novels and fifty-two short stories. That he was still in his sixties, and not older, when Mrs Christie first introduces us to him in *The Mysterious Affair at Styles* is suggested by a remark of Hastings, when he fails to understand Poirot's train of thought: 'The idea crossed my mind, not for the first time, that poor old Poirot was growing old.' If Poirot had appeared to be in his seventies, the *idea* that he might be growing old would probably not have crossed even Hastings' mind.

One of Agatha Christie's great achievements as a crime writer was to make murder cosy enough to be palatable to refined middleclass tastes. She abhorred violence, and those who see in it the only reality will seek that kind of reality in vain in the Christiean *oeuvre*. Her appeal is incredibly wide—*ça va sans dire*, as Poirot might say—and it is an appeal not to the blood lust but to a civilized delight in the puzzle shared by her readers of all social and intellectual classes. One can discuss Agatha Christie novels with cleaning ladies and classical scholars, with dustmen and dons.

This coziness is, of course, in itself unreal. *The Mysterious Affair at Styles* has the inhuman remoteness of the puzzle, but it also, curiously, has something of the texture of a social document as well, especially now, more than half a century after it was written, when its social world has all but disappeared. To Agatha Christie, it would seem to have been already disappearing in 1916. The atmosphere in Styles Court and in the nearby village of Styles St. Mary is of a country at war. The war may be only a lightly sketched background, but it is there. The servants necessary to staff a large country house are there, too, but only just. Of Dorcus, the faithful old family retainer, Hastings says, 'I thought what a fine specimen she was of the old-fashioned servant that is so fast dying out.'

The values implicitly subscribed to, and the opinions expressed by many of her characters, can reasonably be assumed to be shared by the young author of *Styles*. Evidence in a good many of the early Christie novels seems to point to an unthinking, casual anti-semitism of the kind then prevalent in the English upperclasses. In *Styles*, Dr Bauerstein, a Polish Jew, is suspected of spying. 'A very clever man—a Jew of course,' says Poirot, at which Hastings exclaims, 'The blackguard!' Not too worrying, though there is a suggestion that the doctor's Jewish cleverness is as reprehensible as his espionage activities. In any case, the balance is redressed somewhat with this exchange between a jealous husband and his wife who is infatuated with Bauerstein:

> 'I've had enough of the fellow hanging about. He's a Polish Jew, anyway.' 'A tinge of Jewish blood is not a bad thing. It leavens the'—she looked at him—'stolid stupidity of the ordinary Englishman.'

The tactics, though not the actual method of murder, used by the killer of Mrs Inglethorp were adopted successfully by a real-life murderer about ten years after the publication of Agatha Christie's first novel. It is quite possible that he derived his inspiration from a reading of the book. Other odd facts to be noted about *The Mysterious Affair at Styles* are that the author emphasizes the puzzle–solving aspect of the reading experience by including two plans, one of the first floor of Styles Court and one of Mrs Inglethorp's bedroom, and a number of illustrations of clues, letters, fragments of handwriting and cryptic messages; that Hastings gives evidence of his propensity for redheads, which will continue to be displayed in later stories, by unsuccessfully proposing marriage to one; and that Agatha Christie signals to the reader in the final paragraph of the novel that she is prepared to produce one or more sequels to *Styles*. 'Console yourself, my friend,' Poirot says to Hastings who has failed to capture his redhead. 'We may hunt together again, who knows? And then—'

Though her gift for tight and ingenious plotting and her flair for creating believable characters mainly through convincing dialogue were to develop greatly in the next ten or fifteen years, with *The Mysterious Affair at Styles* Mrs Christie made an extraordinarily successful début as a crime writer. Her novel is a distinct improvement on the average level of the genre as it was then practised, and looking back on it more than half a century later you can see that, in fact, it ushered in a new era for the detective story, an era which Agatha Christie would come to dominate with her engaging and fiendishly ingenious puzzles, an era which lasted for more than three decades and which is referred to now as the Golden Age of crime fiction.

The Secret Adversary (1922)

With Archibald and Agatha Christie living in a flat in London, and Agatha's mother still attempting to keep up Ashfield, the Torquay house, on an inadequate income to which Agatha could not afford to contribute, the question of selling Ashfield was raised by Archie. When Agatha received the suggestion with horror, Archie then proposed that she should try to raise funds towards the upkeep of Ashfield by writing another murder mystery. After all, although she had earned only £25 from *The Mysterious Affair at Styles*, it had been well received and had sold a respectable number of copies. The Bodley Head had presumably not lost money on it, and would no doubt be willing to pay a little more for a second novel.

Agatha, apparently, had already begun a second novel, but was not sure whether The Bodley Head would like it. It was not another detective story, but a thriller, so there was no place in it for Hercule Poirot. The idea for the book had first come to her one day in an A.B.C. teashop, one of a chain of London cafés, when she had overheard two people at a nearby table talking about a girl called Jane Fish. That, she thought, would make quite a good beginning: someone overhearing an unusual name in a café, and then remembering it when it came up again in a different context. Jane Fish, however, was perhaps just a little too comical, so Agatha altered it to Jane Finn, and set to work to invent a plot.

Young people in their twenties were being demobilized from the armed forces after the First World War and finding it difficult to settle down to civilian life. Many were unable to find jobs, or were having to act as door-to-door salesmen. Mrs Christie, who found herself frequently answering the doorbell to ex-servicemen, and buying stockings, household gadgets or even poems from them, decided to have such a pair as the young hero and heroine of her thriller.

When she had finished writing her book some months later, Agatha took it to John Lane of The Bodley Head who had published *The Mysterious Affair at Styles* and who had an option on this and her next four books. Lane was disappointed at finding it was not another murder mystery, thought it would sell less well than *Styles*, and even considered rejecting it. In due course, however, The Bodley Head published the novel, which its author decided to call *The Secret Adversary* having first considered *The Joyful Venture* and *The Young Adventurers* (The Young Adventurers Ltd, in fact became the title of Chapter I). The publishers disposed of serial rights to *The Weekly Times*, as they had done with *Styles*, and sold a reasonable number of copies. This time Mrs Christie 'got £50 doled out' to her by John Lane. It was, she considered, encouraging, though not encouraging enough for her to think that she had as yet adopted anything so grand as a profession. She would have been astonished if anyone had told her she would, from now until the end of her life, publish at least one book a year, sometimes one novel and one collection of short stories, sometimes two novels, and in one year (1934) a total of two crime novels, two volumes of short stories and (under a pseudonym) one romantic novel.

With *The Secret Adversary* in 1922, Agatha Christie introduced her readers to two characters whom she would use again in four later novels: *Partners in Crime* (1929), *N or M?* (1941), *By the Pricking of My Thumbs* (1968) and *Postern of Fate* (1974). It is as well, therefore, that Thomas Beresford and Prudence Cowley, known to their friends as Tommy and Tuppence, are only in their twenties in 1922, for this enabled their creator to allow them to age naturally. In their final adventure in 1974 they are presented as an elderly married couple with three grandchildren. When we first meet them, however, in *The Secret Adversary*, they are young, and just emerging from wartime activities, he as a Lieutenant in the army, who had been in action in France, Mesopotamia and Egypt, and she as a maid-of-all-work in an officers' hospital in London. Tuppence is, perhaps, the author as Agatha Christie liked to fantasize herself, and Tommy is the kind of young man who appealed to the fantasy Agatha.

The relationship of the young couple is lightly romantic, though they refrain from confessing their feelings for each other until the last page of *The Secret Adversary*, and their style of speech is positively Wodehousian. 'Tommy, old thing!' and 'Tuppence, old bean!' they exclaim when they meet unexpectedly for the first time since the war, at the exit to the Dover Street tube station. (This is not a fictitious venue: there used to be a Dover Street station on the Piccadilly line.)

Set in 1920, in the autumn and winter of which year it was written, *The Secret Adversary* is dedicated 'To ALL THOSE WHO LEAD MONOTONOUS LIVES in the hope that they may experience at second hand the delights and dangers of adventure'. If, in her first novel, Mrs Christie had set forth one of her two favourite subjects, the murder committed in (or at least involving the members of) an upperclass or upper-middleclass household, in her second she introduces her other favourite, the master criminal seeking to dominate the world. These two themes, domestic crime and global crime, continue to appear throughout her career, though the domestic crime novels not only greatly outnumber the thrillers involving international criminals or crime syndicates, but also are generally considered to be vastly superior to them.

The Secret Adversary begins with a prologue which takes place at 2 P.M. on the afternoon of 7 May 1915, in the Atlantic Ocean off the south coast of Ireland. The *Lusitania* has just been torpedoed by a German submarine, and is sinking fast. Women and children are lining up for the lifeboats, and a man approaches one of the women, an eighteen-year-old girl, to ask if she will take possession of some 'vitally important papers' which may make all the difference to the Allies in the war. The *Lusitania* settles with a more decided list to starboard as the girl goes forward to take her place in the lifeboat, and then suddenly we are in Mayfair, five years later, with Tommy and Tuppence blocking the exit to the Dover Street underground station, turning themselves into the Young Adventurers.

The Prologue is brief, graphic, and flings the reader *in medias res:* the sudden juxtaposition of a grey, grim Atlantic with the bright sunshine of post-war London and the cheerful optimism of the young adventurers, Tommy and Tuppence, is startlingly effective. In the interests of accuracy, however, it should be noted that Mrs Christie thought the *Lusitania* was sunk by two torpedoes. In fact, the German U-boat fired only one torpedo: those among the survivors who may have thought otherwise were misled by secondary explosions from the *Lusitania*'s boilers.

The story proper concerns the efforts of Tommy and Tuppence to trace the girl, Jane Finn, who survived the *Lusitania* disaster only to disappear immediately afterwards with those secret papers which, if they were made public now, months after the end of the war, would cause great embarrassment to the British Government. Mr Carter, a mysterious individual who is very high up in the British Secret Service, recruits the Young Adventurers to save the country. We are left in no doubt of Agatha Christie's political leanings when Mr Carter points out to the Adventurers, Tommy and Tuppence, how vital it is that the documents should be retrieved and suppressed, for they could discredit a number of Conservative statesmen (—was there really a time when a government of any political persuasion contained 'a number of' statesmen?—) and that would never do. 'As a party cry for Labour it would be irresistible, and a Labour Government at this juncture,' Mr Carter adds, 'would, in my opinion, be a grave disability for British trade.'

During the course of their search, Tommy and Tuppence encounter a number of entertaining characters, some of them engaging but others distinctly unsavoury. They include Julius P. Hersheimmer, Jane Finn's American millionaire cousin; Albert, the cockney liftboy in a Mayfair apartment block; and Sir James Peel Edgerton, a distinguished barrister, 'the most celebrated KC in England', a man likely to become a future Prime Minister. What links *The Secret Adversary*, and later Christie thrillers, with the murder mysteries on which the author's reputation most securely rests is the fact that these and a number of other characters whom Tommy and Tuppence find themselves either collaborating with or pitted against are not only the clearcut 'goodies' and 'baddies' of the usual thriller, but are potential suspects as well. For, although Agatha Christie clearly differentiates the thriller from the murder mystery, she retains an element of the puzzle in her thrillers. The question 'Who?' is asked in the thrillers; it is simply that the question 'How?' becomes equally important.

In *The Secret Adversary*, the puzzle is the identity of the adversary. The Bolshevists, we are informed, are behind the labour unrest in the country, but there is a certain man who is '*behind the Bolshevists*' (the italics are Mrs Christie's). 'Who is he?' Mr Carter asks rhetorically:

> 'We do not know. He is always spoken of by the unassuming title of "Mr Brown". But one thing is certain, he is the master criminal of this age. He controls a marvellous organization. Most of the peace propaganda during the war was originated and financed by him. His spies are everywhere.'

Tommy manages to eavesdrop upon a meeting of Mr Brown's organization, at which various representatives report on their activities. A Sinn Feiner guarantees to produce, within a month, 'such a reign of terror in Ireland as shall shake the British Empire to its foundations'. Others have infiltrated the trade unions: the report from the miners is thought to be most satisfactory, but 'we must hold back the railways. There may be trouble with the ASE.' It is important that the principal Labour leaders should have no inkling that they are being used by the Bolshevists. 'They are honest men,' says the representative from Moscow, 'and that is their value to us.'

All good clean reactionary fun, and not without a certain absurd relevance to political life in the 1980s! Those who take their politics solemnly, if anyone other than politicians is still able to do so, will probably reflect that *The Secret Adversary* gives an interestingly distorted picture of the social and industrial unrest which followed the First World War and which, during the years which saw the consolidation of the Russian revolution, was to lead to the General Strike in Great Britain, an event which is curiously anticipated in more than one of Agatha Christie's early novels. But Mrs Christie is politically no further to the right in her thrillers than Ian Fleming in his distinctly less amusing James Bond novels of the nineteen-fifties and sixties.

The villain is unmasked at the end of *The Secret Adversary* and the threatened General Strike is averted or, as we now know, postponed. Inspector Japp has made, not an appearance, but a certain effect offstage, and the reader with a knowledge of nineteenth-century French opera will probably spot a certain clue which will leave those who suffer from amusia (the inability to comprehend or produce musical sounds) mystified.

The Secret Adversary was the first Agatha Christie novel to be made into a film. This did not happen until 1928, by which time Mrs Christie was being published in a number of foreign languages. The film, produced by a German company, was called *Die Abenteuer Gmbh* (Adventures Ltd), was directed by Fred Sauer, and starred Carlo Aldini, Eve Gray and a Russian character actor, Michael or Mikhail Rasumny, who was to appear in a number of Hollywood movies in the nineteen-forties and fifties.

The Murder on the Links (1923)

Archie Christie had a friend, Major Belcher, who was a larger-than-life character with the ability to bluff people into giving him positions of responsibility. Belcher came to dine one evening with the Christies at Earls Court, and explained that he was shortly to leave on a grand tour of the British Empire in order to organize 'this Empire Exhibition we're having in eighteen months' time'. 'The Dominions,' Belcher explained to Archie and Agatha, 'have got to be alerted, to stand on their toes and to cooperate in the whole thing,' and it was Belcher's mission to ensure that they did so. He invited Archie to come with him as financial adviser, with all expenses paid and a fee of £1,000. Agatha would be permitted to accompany the party, since most of the transport was being provided free of charge by the ships and railways of the various Commonwealth countries to be visited.

Archie Christie had already grown tired of his job in the City, and when Belcher announced the proposed itinerary, from South Africa to Australia and New Zealand, then on to Canada after a brief holiday in Honolulu, the Christies agreed to go. Agatha longed to travel and see as much of the world as possible, but had expected that, as the wife of a business man, two weeks abroad each summer would be all she was ever likely to get. There was a certain risk to be taken, for Colonel Christie's employer was not willing to guarantee to keep his job open for him on his return, but the Christies did not consider themselves to be people who played safe. Like Agatha's Tommy and Tuppence, they yearned for adventure and were perfectly willing to take risks. Off they went, around the world with Major Belcher, leaving their daughter with Agatha's sister.

The British Empire Exhibition Mission set off in grand style on the *Kildonan Castle*, bound for Cape Town. But Agatha Christie's enjoyment was soon cut short: the weather in the Bay of Biscay was atrocious, the ship was tossed about violently, and for four days Agatha suffered the most appalling seasickness. The ship's doctor became seriously concerned about her, and a woman in a nearby cabin who had caught a glimpse of her was heard, on the fourth day, to ask the stewardess: 'Is the lady in the cabin opposite dead yet?' However, her condition improved when the ship docked at Madeira, and although she subsequently became ill again whenever the weather was rough at sea, it was never quite as bad as those first days. In due course, the ship reached Cape Town, and Agatha was delighted to be back on *terra firma* for a time.

By now, she had come to know Major Belcher quite well, and to realize that travelling around the world with him was not going to be the entirely happy experience she and Archie had anticipated. The Major was very demanding, complained continually about the service, and bullied his secretary, Mr Bates, a serious, somewhat humourless young man and an excellent secretary, though nature had given him 'the appearance of a villain in a melodrama, with black hair, flashing eyes and an altogether sinister aspect'. 'Looks the complete thug, doesn't he?' Belcher said to the Christies. 'You'd say he was going to cut your throat any moment. Actually he is the most respectable fellow you have ever known.' Neither Belcher nor his secretary realized that they were being scrutinized, analyzed and filed away for future reference by a crime novelist always ready to make use of a colourful character or two.

From Cape Town Agatha travelled on to the diamond mines at Kimberley; to Salisbury and the Victoria Falls; to Livingstone where she saw crocodiles swimming about, and hippopotami; to Johannesburg, Pretoria and Durban. She and Archie managed to do a great deal of surfing at Muizenberg, in Cape Province, before facing the, in her case, dreaded sea voyage to Australia.

In Australia she was fascinated by the parrots, blue and red and green, 'flying through the air in great clustering swarms', and by the gigantic tree ferns in the bush outside Melbourne. The food and the sanitary arrangements left much to be desired, but staying on a sheep station in New South Wales was an unusual and enjoyable experience. In the major cities, Belcher made successful public speeches, or rather repeated the same speech which his travelling companions soon knew by heart. After visiting Tasmania, where Agatha fell in love with 'incredibly beautiful Hobart' and decided to go back and live there one day, the party proceeded to New Zealand.

Belcher had, by now, revealed himself in his true colours. The Christies found him for much of the time to be rude, overbearing, inconsiderate and oddly mean in small matters. He was continually sending Agatha out to buy him white cotton socks and neglecting to pay her for them. He behaved, Agatha remembered later, like a spoilt child, but had such immense charm when he was on his best behaviour that he was instantly forgiven. Tasmania forgotten, Agatha now thought New Zealand the most beautiful country she had ever seen, and vowed to go back one day. (However, by the time that air travel had made it possible to get there quickly, an elderly Agatha Christie had decided that her travelling days were over.)

After a lazy voyage, stopping at Fiji and other islands, Agatha and Archie arrived in Honolulu for two weeks' holiday, while Belcher stayed with friends in New Zealand, after which they all embarked upon the last and most gruelling part of their journey, a tour of Canada. It was from the Banff Springs Hotel in Banff National Park, high up in the Rockies, that Mrs Christie wrote on 26 September 1922, to Basil Willett of The Bodley Head thanking him for a cheque for forty-seven pounds, eighteen shillings and ten pence. (But, in December, back in Torquay, she wrote again asking for accounts to be sent to her, and some weeks later had occasion to point out to Mr Willett that, since he had wrongly calculated the selling price of the American edition of *The Secret Adversary*, the exchange rate being $4.45 to the pound, The Bodley Head owed her two pounds, two shillings and three pence.)

Before setting out on her tour of the Commonwealth, Agatha had virtually completed a third novel, *The Murder on the Links*, the idea for which she derived from newspaper reports of a murder in France. Masked men had broken into a house, killed the owner and left his wife bound and gagged. There were discrepancies in the wife's story, and a suggestion that she may have killed her husband. This led Agatha to invent her own plot, beginning several years later and in a different part of France.

Hercule Poirot having been a decided success on his first appearance, he and Captain Hastings were employed again in *The Murder on the Links*. The Bodley Head professed themselves pleased with the novel, but its author quarrelled with them over the jacket they provided for it. She thought its colours ugly and the actual drawing poor. In her autobiography she claims that the jacket was also misleading in that it appeared to represent a man in pyjamas on a golf-links, dying of an epileptic fit, whereas the character had been fully dressed and stabbed in the back. But, in fact, the murdered man, according to Mrs Christie's text, wore only underclothes beneath an over-coat. Whoever was in the right about the jacket, a certain amount of bad feeling was engendered between author and publisher, and Agatha secured her publisher's agreement that, in future, she should see and approve jacket designs for her books. (She had already had another difference of opinion with her publisher, during the production of her first novel, *The Mysterious Affair at Styles*, over the spelling of the hot drink, cocoa, which Miss Howse, an eccentric employee of the firm and described by Mrs Christie as a dragon, insisted should be spelled 'coco'. Agatha produced dictionaries, tins of cocoa, but failed to make any impression on Miss Howse.)

With *The Murder on the Links*, Agatha Christie returned to the murder mystery or puzzle type of novel, and to her team of Poirot and Hastings. Years later, she wrote of it:

> I think *Murder on the Links* was a moderately good example of
> its kind—though rather melodramatic. This time I provided
> a love affair for Hastings. If I *had* to have a love interest in the
> book, I thought I might as well marry off Hastings. Truth to
> tell, I think I was getting a little tired of him. I might be stuck
> with Poirot, but no need to be stuck with Hastings too.

The Murder on the Links is a more than 'a moderately good' example of its kind. Until the diabolically ingenious solution, which perhaps fails to convince because of its very complexity, the action moves swiftly, the small seaside resort on the northern coast of France rings true and is not simply an

English village in disguise, and the characters, lightly sketched though they are, all come vividly to life. The skill with which Agatha Christie manipulates her plot involving two crimes committed twenty years apart is quite brilliant. Occasionally, however, she displays an odd carelessness in matters of detail. For instance, the corpse of the murdered man is described when it is viewed by Poirot and Hastings. The face is clean-shaven, the nose thin, the eyes set rather close together, and the skin bronzed. We are told that the dead man's 'lips were drawn back from his teeth and an expression of absolute amazement and terror was stamped on the livid features'. The features, it is clear, are at least intact and undamaged. But Poirot finds a short piece of lead piping which, according to him, was used to 'disfigure the victim's face so that it would be unrecognizable'. Poirot's theory of the crime, fortunately, does not hinge upon this point!

Since we are in France, Inspector Japp of Scotland Yard is not available to act as a foil for Poirot. This function is undertaken by Giraud, a young detective from the Sûreté who is already famous and inclined to pour scorn on Poirot's old-fashioned methods. Agatha Christie has confessed that, in writing *The Murder on the Links*, she was influenced less by the Sherlock Holmes stories than by Gaston Leroux's *The Mystery of the Yellow Room*. She must also have been reading A.E.W. Mason's *At the Villa Rose*, for certain events at the Villa Geneviève in *The Murder on the Links* call the 1910 mystery classic to mind.

Since their earlier adventure in Essex, Poirot and Hastings have taken furnished rooms together in London. If you did not learn from *The Big Four* (1927) that their address was 14 Farraway Street, you would have sworn that it was 221B Baker Street, for the ambience is distinctly Holmesian, as is their landlady, who is difficult to distinguish from Sherlock Holmes's Mrs Hudson. Captain Hastings works as private secretary to a Member of Parliament while Poirot pursues a retirement career as private detective, and Hastings finds time to write up Poirot's cases, just as Watson used to chronicle those of Holmes. At the end of *The Murder on the Links*, it seems likely that Hastings will propose marriage to the auburn-haired beauty he has met, and there is even a hint that he, or they, may emigrate to 'a ranch across the seas'. Mrs Christie, it would seem, was already laying her plans for the removal of Hastings from Poirot's life.

The Man in the Brown Suit (1924)

Back in London after their world tour, the Christies for a time found it difficult to settle down. Agatha longed for a cottage in the country, near enough to town for Archie to commute to the city, but far enough away for little Rosalind to be able to breathe air fresher than that of Earl's Court. Archie took some months to find a job that suited him. Eventually, however, he was offered an excellent position with Austral Trust Ltd, a city firm run by an Australian friend, Clive Baillieu. Archie was to remain with Austral Trust Ltd for the rest of his life. Now, while they searched for their place in the country, Agatha proceeded to work on her next novel.

The egregious Belcher had suggested to her, before they went on their trip, that his house, the Mill House at Dorney, would make an excellent setting for a murder. 'The Mystery of the Mill House,' he had said to her one evening when the Christies were dining there. 'Jolly good title, don't you think?' Agatha admitted that it had possibilities, and on their voyage to Cape Town Major Belcher continued to refer to it. 'But mind you,' he added, 'if you write it you must put me in it.' Agatha doubted if she could manage to create a character based entirely on someone she knew, but Belcher continued to pester her throughout their world tour. When he asked her, for the umpteenth time, 'Have you begun that book yet? Am I in it?' she replied 'Yes. You're the victim.'

But Belcher did not see himself as one of life's victims. 'You've got to make me the murderer, Agatha. Do you understand?' And Mrs Christie replied carefully, 'I understand that you *want* to be the murderer.' She had not, in fact, begun writing the book, but she did sketch out its plot while she was in South Africa, and Belcher played a leading role. 'Give him a title,' Archie suggested. 'He'd like that.' So Belcher became Sir Eustace Pedler. Agatha Christie explained later that Sir Eustace Pedler was not really meant to be Belcher,

> but he used several of Belcher's phrases, and told some of Belcher's stories. He too was a master of the art of bluff, and behind the bluff could easily be sensed an unscrupulous and interesting character. Soon I had forgotten Belcher and had Sir Eustace Pedler himself wielding the pen. It is, I think, the only time I have tried to put a real person whom I knew well into a book, and I don't think it succeeded. Belcher didn't come to life, but someone called Sir Eustace Pedler did. I suddenly found that the book was becoming rather fun to write. I only hoped The Bodley Head would approve of it.

The book was written in London and, retitled *The Man in the Brown Suit* since its author thought the title proposed by Belcher too similar to her earlier ones, was delivered to The Bodley Head who 'hemmed and hawed a bit' because it was not a proper detective story but one of those thrillers which Mrs Christie seemed to find easier to write. However, they accepted it.

Agatha Christie, author of four books, was no longer the novice who had grasped eagerly the chance to have her first novel published. As she herself put it, though she had been ignorant and foolish when she first submitted a book for publication, she had since learned a few things. She had discovered the Society of Authors and read its periodical, from which she learned that you had to be extremely careful in making contracts with publishers, 'and especially with certain publishers'. When The Bodley Head, who still had an option on her next two books after *The Man in the Brown Suit*, suggested shortly before it's publication that they scrap the old contract and make a new one for a further five books, Mrs Christie politely declined. She considered that they had not treated a young and inexperienced author fairly, but had taken advantage of her ignorance of publishers' contracts and her understandable eagerness to have her first book published.

It was at this point that Agatha Christie decided she needed a literary agent and went back to the firm of Hughes Massie. Massie, who had advised her years earlier, had since died, and she was received by a young man with a slight stammer, whose name was Edmund Cork. Finding him impressive, and considerably less alarming than Hughes Massie himself had been, Mrs Christie placed her literary career, such as it was, in Cork's hands, and left his office feeling that an enormous weight had been lifted from her shoulders. It was the beginning of a friendship which lasted for more than fifty years until her death. Edmund Cork has now retired from Hughes Massie Ltd, but the firm still represents the Agatha Christie Literary Estate.

The Evening News offered what seemed to Agatha Christie the unbelievable sum of £500 for the serial rights of *The Man in the Brown Suit*, which she hastily accepted, deciding not to object that the newspaper intended to call the serial version 'Anna the Adventuress', as silly a title as she had ever heard. That she should receive such a huge amount of money, was, she thought, an extraordinary stroke of luck and, when Archie suggested she buy a car with it, Agatha invested in a grey, bottle-nosed Morris Cowley which, she revealed many years later, was the first of the two most exciting things in her life. (The second was her invitation to dine with Queen Elizabeth II at Buckingham Palace many years later.)

The Man in the Brown Suit, another of the thrillers which Agatha Christie found easier and 'more fun' to write than her detective stories, is one of her best in that genre. The heroine, Anne Beddingfield, is a romantic young woman whose archaeologist father dies, leaving her little more than the opportunity to be free and to seek adventure. Adventure, for Anne, begins when she witnesses the apparently accidental death of a man who falls onto the electrified rails at Hyde Park Corner tube station. Finding reason to suspect that the man's death was not accidental, Anne persuades the great newspaper magnate Lord Nasby, 'millionaire owner of the *Daily Budget*' and several other papers, to commission her to investigate the matter. (For Nasby, we are probably meant to read Northcliffe.) A second death occurs at the Mill House, Marlow, whose owner is Sir Eustace Pedler, MP, and the trail leads Anne to sail to Cape Town on the *Kilmorden Castle*. On board, she meets Sir Eustace, a character whom Agatha Christie, as we know, based largely on Major Belcher, and his secretary, Guy Pagett, who, like the real life secretary of Belcher, 'has the face of a fourteenth century poisoner'. Anne, like Agatha herself, proves to be a very poor sailor, and it is not until they reach Madeira that she begins to feel she might possibly recover from her seasickness.

With the exception of a Prologue set in Paris, the entire action of the novel takes place either *en route* to, or in South Africa and Rhodesia, and is presented through the diaries of Anne and Sir Eustace. The villain is a master criminal who organizes crime 'as another man might organize a boot factory'. Jewel robberies, forgery, espionage, assassination, he has dabbled in them all. He is known to his underlings simply as 'the Colonel', and it falls to Anne finally to unmask him, with the aid of two or three friends.

Who Anne's friends are, and who her enemies, is something which Mrs Christie keeps her readers guessing about. Like all Christie thrillers, *The Man in the Brown Suit* incorporates the puzzle element into its plot as well. Thus it retains a hold on the loyalties of those who prefer the murder mystery to the thriller, for it conceals until the last pages the identity of 'the Colonel' (who is, after all, a murderer), while at the same time including all the ingredients of the 'international crime' story: action, violence, suspense. Whether or not the charming old rogue Sir Eustace Pedler is at all like Major Belcher, he is one of Agatha Christie's most convincing and memorable characters, and the author's underestimated ability to convey a strong sense of place is very much in evidence in her discreet but effective description of the exotic African landscape through which Pedler, Anne and the others move.

It might be thought that to present the narrative through the diaries of two characters detracts somewhat from the suspense, or at least from the list of suspects. But with Agatha Christie you cannot always be certain that anyone is above suspicion. Diaries can also be published posthumously. (This is not necessarily a clue.) In *The Man in the Brown Suit* Mrs Christie makes use of a device which, to a certain extent, anticipates her tactics in *The Murder of Roger Ackroyd* (1926), though less spectacularly.

It need not impair enjoyment of the novel to know that one of the characters, a strong silent man called Colonel Race, will appear in three later Agatha
Christie novels, ageing over forty years in the process. In fact, enjoyment of *The
Man in the Brown Suit* will be impaired only if you take too seriously the African
revolution which seems to be trying to foment itself offstage. Mrs Christie,
never an acute political observer, rather charmingly recalls in her autobiography
that 'there was some kind of a revolutionary crisis on while we were there, and
I noted down a few useful facts.' Those facts must have got lost somewhere.

Poirot Investigates (1924)

One of Hercule Poirot's earliest fans was Bruce Ingram, editor of the
London illustrated weekly, *The Sketch*. Ingram got in touch with Agatha
Christie to suggest that she should write a series of Hercule Poirot stories for
his magazine, and a thrilled and delighted Agatha agreed. She was not
entirely pleased with the drawing of Hercule Poirot which *The Sketch*
commissioned to accompany the first of the stories: it was not unlike her idea
of Poirot but it made him look a little too smart and dandified. Agatha
Christie wrote eight stories, and at first it was thought that eight would be
sufficient. However, it was eventually decided to extend the series to twelve,
and the author had to produce another four rather too hastily. When the
series of stories began, in the 7 March 1923 issue of *The Sketch*, it was accompanied by a page of photographs of 'The Maker of "The Grey Cells of M.
Poirot"', showing her at home with her daughter, in her drawing-room, on
the telephone, at her writing table, at work with her typewriter and so on.

The author of 'the thrilling set of detective yarns' made it clear to The
Bodley Head that she thought they should publish them quickly as a volume
of stories, while the publicity from their appearance in *The Sketch* and from
the serialization of *The Man in the Brown Suit* in the London *Evening News*
was still current. The Bodley Head agreed, and the stories were collected in
a volume which, at first, it was intended should be called *The Grey Cells of
Monsieur Poirot*, but which, in due course, appeared as *Poirot Investigates*. The
volume was also published in the United States (by Dodd, Mead & Co, who
remain Agatha Christie's American hardback publishers), but there is a
discrepancy between the British and American editions. The British volume
consisted of eleven stories while the American edition contained fourteen.
(The three extra stories, 'The Lost Mine', 'The Chocolate Box' and 'The
Veiled Lady' eventually appeared in Great Britain, along with several other
stories, fifty years later in *Poirot's Early Cases*. 'The Veiled Lady' was also
published, together with two other stories, in *Poirot Lends a Hand*.)

Some, though not many, of Agatha Christie's short stories are as satisfying as the best of her novels. In general, however, her talent is not suited to the short story; or at least not to the very short mystery story of which she wrote so many. Her plots are, perforce, skeletal, and her characterization at its most perfunctory. The puzzle element is, therefore, given even greater emphasis than in the novels in which it contributes largely to the reader's pleasure. Many of the stories, including most of the Hercule Poirot adventures collected in *Poirot Investigates*, are little more than puzzles or tricks given 'a local habitation and a name'.

Prior to the emergence of Agatha Christie upon the crime writers' scene, many of the genre's greatest successes were with short stories. It is generally agreed, for instance, that Conan Doyle's Sherlock Holmes stories are superior to the Holmes novels, and most of the other mystery writers who flourished at the same time as Conan Doyle, among them G.K. Chesterton (with his Catholic priest detective Father Brown), Baroness Orczy, Richard Austin Freeman (whose detective was the physician Dr. John Thorndyke), the American Melville Davisson Post (whose mysteries are solved by Uncle Abner, a shrewd Virginian), H.C. Bailey with his Mr Fortune stories, and Ernest Bramah, all produced their most successful work in the form of the short story. However, though she wrote more than a hundred and fifty short stories, Agatha Christie's greatest triumphs were to be achieved with her full-length novels, rather than with short stories or novellas.

That so many of Agatha Christie's stories are little more than puzzles or tricks might not matter so much were the puzzles more varied and the tricks less repetitive. For instance, the first time that Poirot points the accusing finger accurately at the person who engaged him, the reader is surprised and delighted; but M. Poirot and Mrs Christie connive several times at this particular trick, which is also not unknown in the novels.

The stories in *Poirot Investigates* are, on their own level, quite entertaining, but it would be as unwise to read more than one or two at a sitting as it would be to consume a two-pound box of chocolates in one go. Occasionally, Mrs Christie's touch falters, as when, in 'The Adventure of the Italian Nobleman' she is snide about Inspector Japp's French accent and has him refer to the 'boat train to the *Continong*'. Why would he not pronounce 'continent' as an English word? But usually her social placing is exact. In 'The Case of the Missing Will', Poirot's client, a handsome young woman, explains that her father, who came of farming stock, 'married slightly above him; my mother was the daughter of a poor artist.'

'The Adventure of the Egyptian Tomb', in which Poirot investigates a strange series of deaths of people who were involved in the discovery and opening of the tomb of King Men-her-Ra, an event which we are told followed hard upon the discovery of the tomb of Tutankhamun by Lord Carnarvon, is interesting as evidence that Agatha Christie was conversant with the science of archaeology some years before she met Max Mallowan. (She had already introduced an archaeologist into her collection of characters in *The Man in the Brown Suit.*)

One of the best stories in *Poirot Investigates* is 'The Kidnapped Prime Minister'. It is also one in which we learn something more of the author's political opinions, or opinions which it seems reasonably safe to attribute to the author even though she issues them through the mouths of her characters and not by way of authorial comment. It is unlikely that, in 1923, any irony was intended in the opening sentence of the story (even a story narrated by the not very shrewd Hastings), which begins, 'Now that war and the problems of war are things of the past . . .' But pacifism takes a knocking at more than one point in the story, and the statement made by someone meant to be a leading British politician that 'the Pacifist propaganda, started and maintained by the German agents in our midst, has been very active' seems to be accepted by Poirot and Hastings without modification. The politician is 'Lord Estair, Leader of the House of Commons'. Is it, in fact, possible for a nobleman to lead the House of Commons? Apparently, if his is a courtesy title.

It is in 'The Kidnapped Prime Minister' that Poirot most clearly describes his method. He has declined to leap into a military car at Boulogne and set off in pursuit of the kidnappers:

> He shot a quick glance at us. 'It is not so that the good detective should act, eh? I perceive your thought. He must be full of energy. He must rush to and fro. He should prostrate himself on the dusty road and seek the marks of tyres through a little glass. He must gather up the cigarette-end, the fallen match? That is your idea, is it not?'
>
> His eyes challenged us. 'But I—Hercule Poirot—tell you that it is not so! The true clues are within—*here!*' He tapped his forehead. 'See you, I need not have left London. It would have been sufficient for me to sit quietly in my rooms there. All that matters is the little grey cells within. Secretly and silently they do their part, until suddenly I call for a map, and I lay my finger on a spot—so—and I say: the Prime Minister is *there!* and it is so!'

Nevertheless, when it suits him Poirot is not at all averse to snooping about, gathering up the cigarette-end and the fallen match. He has sufficient confidence and vanity to contradict himself whenever he feels like it. In these early stories, he is at his most Holmesian, and the parallels with the minutiae of the Conan Doyle stories are most noticeable. Hastings, similarly, has become more Watsonian than ever, and in some of the stories Mrs Christie treats his relationship with Poirot mechanically. In addition to the stories already mentioned, the volume contains 'The Adventure of "The Western Star"', 'The Tragedy at Marsdon Manor', 'The Adventure of the Cheap Flat', 'The Mystery of Hunter's Lodge', 'The Million Dollar Bond Robbery', 'The Jewel Robbery at the *Grand Metropolitan*' and 'The Disappearance of Mr Davenheim'.

The Road of Dreams (1924)

Ever since she was a child, Agatha Christie had written poetry. One of her earliest efforts, written at the age of eleven, begins: 'I knew a little cowslip and a pretty flower too,/Who wished she was a bluebell and had a robe of blue.' In her teens, she had occasional poems published in magazines, and by the time she was in her mid-thirties there were enough of them to be gathered into a slim volume which, in 1924, the London publishing house of Geoffrey Bles published, under the title of *The Road of Dreams*. This was also the title of one of the poems in the volume ('The Road of Dreams leads up the Hill/So straight and white/And bordered wide/With almond trees on either side/In rosy flush of Spring's delight! . . .')

Agatha Christie's talent for poetry was genuine, but modest and of no startling originality: the finest poetry is made not out of feelings but out of words, and Agatha Christie was not sufficiently in love with words to become a poet of real distinction. She did, however, enjoy relieving her feelings in verse and, in doing so, occasionally produced a pleasant little lyric poem.

The Road of Dreams is divided into four sections. The first, 'A Masque from Italy', is a sequence of nine poems or 'songs' to be performed by the *commedia dell' arte* characters, Harlequin and Columbine, Pierrot and Pierrette, Punchinello and Pulcinella. Written when Agatha was in her late teens, the Harlequin poems have a certain wistfulness which is appealing. They are of interest, too, in that they anticipate the Harlequin element which was later to creep into some of her short stories, those involving that mysterious character Mr Harley Quin.

The second section of the volume, 'Ballads', consists of six poems, among them 'Elizabeth of England' ('I am Mistress of England—the Seas I hold!/I have gambled, and won, alone. . .'), which is presumably one of the author's teenage efforts, and 'Ballad of the Maytime', a fey little ballad about bluebells which Mrs Christie wrote in 1924 in Sunningdale.

One or two of the eight poems in 'Dreams and Fantasies', the third section of the volume, are romantically death-obsessed—Keats' 'La belle dame sans merci' is not too far away—and one of them, 'Down in the Wood', which forty years later Mrs Christie still liked sufficiently to reprint in her autobiography, is rather good, with a last line that lingers in the memory: 'And Fear—naked Fear passes out of the wood!' The volume's final section, 'Other Poems', consists of thirteen poems written at various times, about the passing of love, the horror of war and the romance of the unknown. Again, there is a certain amount of evidence that the poet is 'half in love with easeful death':

> Give me my hour within my Lover's arms!
> Vanished the doubts, the fears, the sweet alarms!
> I lose myself within his quickening Breath. . . .
> *And when he tires and leaves me—there is Death . . .*

Mystery is never completely absent from any aspect of Agatha Christie's world, and there are one or two minor mysteries connected with this innocuous volume. The crime writer Michael Gilbert in an article on Agatha Christie mentions the volume's title poem, 'The Road of Dreams', and quotes two stanzas from it. But the stanzas he quotes are part of a completely different poem in the volume, a poem called 'In a Dispensary' which Agatha Miller wrote in her mid-twenties when she was working in the hospital dispensary in Torquay.

Mystery number two is provided by the author of a book described as 'an intimate biography of the first lady of crime' who says that Agatha Christie exposed her love for Max Mallowan 'for all the world to see in a poem entitled "To M.E.L.M. in Absence" in *The Road of Dreams* (1924)'. But there is no such poem in *The Road of Dreams*, and Agatha Christie did not meet Max Mallowan until several years after 1924: to be precise, in 1930.

A stanza from 'In a Dispensary' which is not quoted in Michael Gilbert's article clearly reveals the future crime writer's interest in the poisons on the dispensary shelves among which she worked:

> From the Borgia's time to the present day, their power has
>   been proved and tried!
> Monkshead blue, called Aconite, and the deadly Cyanide!
> Here is sleep and solace and soothing of pain—courage and
>   vigour new!
> Here is menace and murder and sudden death!—in these
>   phials of green and blue!

The final poem in the volume is 'Pierrot Grown Old', which reads as though it ought to have been part of the *commedia dell' arte* sequence, 'A Masque from Italy', with which *The Road of Dreams* begins. (When the contents of *The Road of Dreams* were reprinted in *Poems* nearly fifty years later, 'Pierrot Grown Old' was, in fact, taken into the 'Masque' sequence.)

The Secret of Chimneys (1925)

Archie and Agatha did not find the cottage in the country for which they were searching. Instead, they took a flat in a large Victorian country house, which had been divided into four flats. The house, Scotswood, was at Sunningdale in Berkshire, only twenty-four miles from London and close to the Sunningdale Golf Club of which Archie had become a member. Golf was such a passion with Colonel Christie that before long Mrs Christie began to fear she was turning into 'that well-known figure, a golf widow'. She consoled herself by writing *The Secret of Chimneys*, which she later described as 'light-hearted and rather in the style of *The Secret Adversary*'.

Before leaving London for the country, Agatha had taken lessons in sculpture. She was a great admirer of the art, much more than of painting, and was disappointed when she became aware that she possessed no real talent for it. 'By way of vanity', she composed a few songs instead. Her musical education in Paris had been thorough and there had been a moment in her life when she even considered taking up the career of a professional pianist. She also had a pleasant singing voice, so it was appropriate that she should turn, however briefly, to the composition of songs, and equally appropriate that she should set some of her own verses to music. In later years, she continued to profess herself quite pleased with one group of songs in particular, settings of her Pierrot and Harlequin verses. She realized, however, that writing seemed to be the trade to which she was best suited.

After a few months at Scotswood, the Christies decided that they needed a house of their own, and they began to look at properties in the vicinity of Sunningdale. Their choice fell upon a large house with a pleasant garden, and, in 1925, after less than two years in their flat in the country, they moved into their own country house which, at Archie's suggestion, they named Styles after the house in *The Mysterious Affair at Styles*.

Agatha's literary agent, Edmund Cork, had been busy extricating his client from her involvement with The Bodley Head. Cork approached the firm of Collins who had begun to add detective novels to their list, and offered them the first Agatha Christie title which did not have contractually to be offered to The Bodley Head. A three-book contract was signed with

Collins as early as 27 January 1924, though there were at that time two volumes still to be published by The Bodley Head. *The Secret of Chimneys* was the last Agatha Christie novel to appear under The Bodley Head's imprint. Collins became her English publishers for the rest of the author's life.

The Secret of Chimneys is one of the best of Agatha Christie's early thrillers. It is, in its way, as typical of its time, the twenties, as Michael Arlen's *The Green Hat* or P.G. Wodehouse's *The Inimitable Jeeves*, both of which were published several months before *Chimneys*. It also owes something to the Ruritanian world of Anthony Hope's *The Prisoner of Zenda*, for its plot is concerned with political events in the fictitious small Balkan state of Herzoslovakia, the character of whose people appears to be of an almost Montenegran fierceness. After a beginning in Bulawayo, however, the events of the novel take place not in the Balkans but in London or at Chimneys, one of the stately homes of England and the seat of the ninth Marquis of Caterham. Chimneys, we are told, is as much a national possession as a grand country house, and history has been made at its informal weekend parties. It was perhaps not unlike Cliveden.

Diplomatic intrigue involving the possible reinstatement of the Herzoslovakian royal family and international crime concerning the attempts of a jewel thief known throughout Europe as 'King Victor' are ingeniously combined in *The Secret of Chimneys*, and at the end two characters are unmasked and revealed in their true colours, though only one of them is a criminal.

It is when she is freed of some of the restrictions of the domestic murder mystery, as in this type of novel, that Mrs Christie seems able to relax into more leisurely, and, therefore, more detailed and believable characterization. Believable, that is, in the context of your willingly suspended disbelief; for, although the reader greatly enjoys making the acquaintance of, for instance, Baron Lolopretjzyl who represents in London the Loyalist Party of Herzoslovakia, it has to be admitted that the Baron's construction of English sentences is a trifle more exotic than it need be. 'Of many secrets he the knowledge had. Should he reveal but the quarter of them, Europe into war plunged may be,' he says of a fellow countryman.

The Baron resides in a suite at Harridge's Hotel. Mrs Christie's London hotels are only lightly disguised. Mr Anthony Cade, who may or may not be the hero of the story, stays at the Blitz, which seems an inappropriate, indeed irreverent, name for an hotel clearly based on the Ritz. The Blitz, however, is oddly situated. Although, at one point, it appears to be where it ought to be, in Piccadilly, when Anthony Cade first arrives he strolls outside for a brief walk on the Embankment, for all the world as though he were staying at the Savoy.

Though it is not he but one of the upperclass amateurs who solves the secret of Chimneys, Superintendent Battle who is in charge of the case is no plodding and unimaginative policeman inserted into the plot to be the butt of the amateur genius's humour. Battle is not at all like Inspector Japp (who is mentally continually trailing along some steps behind Hercule Poirot's thought processes): he is an intelligent and successful officer whose speciality appears to be crimes in which politics or international diplomacy are involved. Outwardly a stolid and impassive figure, Battle reaches his conclusions by a dogged application of common sense. After *The Secret of Chimneys*, he was to appear in four more Christie novels in some of which he would deal with purely domestic crimes.

Occasionally, Agatha Christie carried over from one book to another characters other than her detectives and policemen. Not only Superintendent Battle but also four other characters from *The Secret of Chimneys* appear again four years later in *The Seven Dials Mystery*, as does the house, Chimneys. The house itself, and the kind of life lived in it, plays a lively part in both novels. Chroniclers of a fast disappearing scene will be interested to note that the lavish English breakfast was still very much in evidence in the twenties. On the sideboard in the dining-room were half a score of heavy silver dishes,'ingeniously kept hot by patent arrangements'. Lord Caterham lifts each lid in turn. 'Omelette,' he mutters, 'eggs and bacon, kidneys, devilled bird, haddock, cold ham, cold pheasant.' Deciding he cares for none of these things, he tells his butler to 'ask the cook to poach me an egg.'

The mandatory racial slurs occur in *The Secret of Chimneys*, though apparently they have been edited out of more recent American editions. 'Dagos will be dagos', 'Like all dagos, he couldn't swim', and other remarks are cheerfully exchanged, and of course all references to Jews are uncomplimentary. People are beginning to be interested in Herzoslovakia, Anthony Cade tells his friend Jimmy, and, when asked what kind of people, he replies, 'Hebraic people. Yellow-faced financiers in city offices.' When we meet one of these financiers, Herman Isaacstein, we are invited to smile at Lord Caterham's references to him as 'Mr Ikey Isaacstein', 'Noseystein', and 'Fat Ikey'. But the true-blue British unemployed are treated with equal contempt. When Anthony Cade disguises himself as an out-of-work ex-serviceman, the upperclass Virginia Revel takes one look at him and decides that he is 'a more pleasing specimen than usual of London's unemployed'.

Her attitude to democracy is so unsympathetic, at least as expressed by a character of whom Mrs Christie evidently approves, that it reveals an unexpectedly authoritarian aspect of the author's nature:

Mind you, I still believe in democracy. But you've got to force
it on people with a strong hand—ram it down their throats.
Men don't want to be brothers—they may some day, but they
don't now. My belief in the brotherhood of man died the day
I arrived in London last week, when I observed the people
standing in a Tube train resolutely refuse to move up and
make room for those who entered. You won't turn people
into angels by appealing to their better natures yet awhile—
but by judicious force you can coerce them into behaving
more or less decently to one another to go on with.

It is true that people on the Moscow underground are less surly in
their behaviour than those in London and New York, but you would hesitate to use the citizenry of Moscow as a kind of democratic barometer.
Even Agatha Christie, one imagines, if she had been offered the choice
would have preferred to be bad-tempered in a democracy than polite in a
police state.

The danger of pontificating solemnly on the subject of Agatha
Christie's politics must, however, be guarded against. The author tells us in
The Secret of Chimneys that there was nothing that bored Lord Caterham
more than politics, unless it was politicians, and one suspects that she
shared his Lordship's feelings. No one need be deterred from enjoying *The
Secret of Chimneys* by Agatha Christie's politics, nor even by occasional infe-
licities in her prose style, though prose is more serious a matter than politics. Is there not something endearing about an author who can write the
phrase, 'eyeing a taxi that was crawling past with longing eyes'?

In general, Mrs Christie's grasp of style is firm: *The Secret of Chimneys* is
enjoyable because its style is light and humorous. It is not, like Anthony Hope's
The Prisoner of Zenda, an adventure-romance, but a comedy-adventure, which
is perhaps a new category.

The Murder of Roger Ackroyd (1926)

It seems now to be generally accepted that the basic idea for *The Murder of
Roger Ackroyd* was given to Agatha Christie by Lord Mountbatten. Mountbatten certainly continued to claim, on every possible occasion, that this was
so. But a variant of the idea, whether you regard it as an outrageous fraud or
remarkably original or both, had earlier been suggested by Mrs Christie's
brother-in-law, James Watts, and the author was already mulling it over. It
appealed greatly to her, but before starting to write the novel she had to work

out just how to make use of the startling suggestion (which will not be revealed in these pages), in such a way that it could not be regarded as cheating the reader. Of course, as Mrs Christie was to admit in her autobiography, a number of people do consider themselves cheated when they come to the end of *The Murder of Roger Ackroyd*, but if they read it carefully they will see that they are wrong, for 'such little lapses of time as there have to be are nicely concealed in an ambiguous sentence'.

It was with *The Murder of Roger Ackroyd*, by far the most ingenious crime novel she had written, that Agatha Christie's reputation took a great leap forward, and so did her sales. The author's solution to the mystery is still debated in books and articles on crime fiction, more than half a century after the novel's first publication, and although its immediate success meant no more than that an edition of approximately five thousand copies sold out, *The Murder of Roger Ackroyd* must by now have sold well over a million copies.

Critics and readers were divided on the propriety of Mrs Christie's brilliant trick. Though the *Daily Sketch* thought it 'the best thriller ever', the *News Chronicle* considered *The Murder of Roger Ackroyd* a 'tasteless and unfortunate let-down by a writer we had grown to admire'. One reader wrote a letter to *The Times* in which he announced that, having been a great admirer of Agatha Christie, he was so shocked by the dénouement of *Roger Ackroyd* that he proposed 'in the future not to buy any more of her books'. Even some of her fellow crime novelists thought she had not played fair, though Dorothy L. Sayers, author of a number of detective novels featuring Lord Peter Wimsey as investigator, defended Mrs Christie by pointing out that 'it's the reader's business to suspect everybody'.

Agatha Christie herself remained unrepentant. In an interview with Francis Wyndham in 1966, she explained: 'I have a certain amount of rules. No false words must be uttered by me. To write "Mrs Armstrong walked home wondering who had committed the murder" would be unfair if she had done it herself. But it's not unfair to leave things out. In *Roger Ackroyd* . . . there's lack of explanation there, but no false statement. Whoever my villain is, it has to be someone I feel *could* do the murder.'

Lord Mountbatten's claim to be responsible for having given Agatha Christie the idea for *Roger Ackroyd* should probably be taken with a pinch of salt. It is true that, at Christmas in 1969, he received from the author a copy of the book, inscribed: 'To Lord Mountbatten in grateful remembrance of a letter he wrote to me forty-five years ago which contained the suggestion which I subsequently used in a book called *The Murder of Roger Ackroyd*. Here once more is my thanks.' However, this was in response to a letter from Mountbatten reminding her that he had written to her forty-five years earlier.

Whether Agatha Christie thought *Roger Ackroyd* her best book is uncertain, but she usually mentioned it as among her three or four favourites.

In *The Murder of Roger Ackroyd*, dedicated not to Lord Mountbatten but 'to PUNKIE, who likes an orthodox detective story, murder, inquest, and suspicion falling on every one in turn!', Agatha Christie returned to the classical domestic crime novel for the first time since *Murder on the Links* three years earlier, and at the same time reintroduced Hercule Poirot who, apart from the short stories in *Poirot Investigates*, had also been missing for three years.

The story, narrated not by Poirot's usual associate, Hastings, but by the local doctor whose name is Sheppard, begins with the death of someone other than Roger Ackroyd. Mrs Ferrars, a wealthy widow, has been found dead in her bed, and Dr Sheppard has been sent for. He suspects suicide, but sees no point in saying so publicly. The following evening Roger Ackroyd, a wealthy widower whom village gossip had prophesied would marry Mrs Ferrars, is murdered in the study of his house.

We are soon introduced to Dr Sheppard's sister Caroline who keeps house for him, and to the Sheppards' neighbour, a recent arrival in the village of King's Abbot. He is a foreign gentleman with 'an egg-shaped head, partially covered with suspiciously black hair, two immense moustaches, and a pair of watchful eyes'. He has retired from whatever his profession may have been, grows vegetable marrows, and is thought to be called Porrott.

Porrott, of course, is simply the King's Abbot pronunciation of Poirot, and soon the retired detective has introduced himself to Dr Sheppard, has admitted how bored he is with his vegetable marrows, and how much he misses his friend ('who for many years never left my side') who is now living in the Argentine. When Poirot is asked to investigate the murder of Roger Ackroyd, he allows Dr Sheppard to take the place of his old friend Hastings as assistant and part confidant; and also as Boswell to Poirot's Johnson, for it is Sheppard who writes up the case and is the chronicler of Poirot's eventual success.

It is not a success which comes easily to Poirot, for the suspects are many and varied. Most of them were staying in Ackroyd's house when he was murdered. Major Blunt, a big-game hunter, is an old friend, and appears to have a romantic interest in Ackroyd's niece, Flora. Flora and her mother, who is Ackroyd's widowed sister-in-law, are poor relations living on a rich man's charity. Geoffrey Raymond, the dead man's secretary, Ursula Bourne, a somewhat unusual parlourmaid, and Ralph Paton, Ackroyd's adopted son who is burdened with gambling debts, all come under suspicion.

Poirot is assisted not only by Dr Sheppard but by the doctor's sister Caroline, a middle-aged spinster who seems to know everything that goes on in the village. Many years later, in discussing the character of Miss Marple, an unconventional solver of puzzles whom she was to introduce in *Murder at the Vicarage*, Agatha Christie said she thought it possible that Miss Marple 'arose from the pleasure I had taken in portraying Dr Sheppard's sister in *The Murder of Roger Ackroyd*. She had been my favourite character in the book— an acidulated spinster, full of curiosity, knowing everything, hearing everything: the complete detective service in the home.'

It is not simply because of its startling dénouement that *The Murder of Roger Ackroyd* has remained one of Agatha Christie's most popular novels. The story is believable, the characters convincing, and Mrs Christie's ear for dialogue is accurate. That she can occasionally be clumsy ought not to obscure the fact that, on form, she writes speech which sounds natural, whether it issues from the mouth of a peeress or a parlourmaid. Even more impressive is her ability to enter into the thought processes of her male characters. Dr Sheppard, the narrator of *Roger Ackroyd*, is a fully rounded and perfectly convincing character, and his loving, exasperated relationship with his sister Caroline, an amusing and acutely observed character, is beautifully conveyed. Another important ingredient in the success of the novel is the background of English village life which Mrs Christie provides. It is never obtrusive but it is there, and it is important.

From *The Murder of Roger Ackroyd* onwards, Agatha Christie's readers knew what to expect, or rather knew that they would never know what to expect. And it is this quality of unexpectedness which makes Mrs Christie unique among crime writers. Dorothy L. Sayers writes more elegantly but also, at times, more ploddingly. Her stories do not move quickly. Ngaio Marsh is in the Christie tradition but can get bogged down in endless interviews with suspects. Patricia Wentworth is pastiche Christie and her villains can usually be guessed. After the trick she played on her public in *Roger Ackroyd* (though some of those who remembered *The Man in the Brown Suit* ought perhaps not to have been taken in), clearly there were no holds barred. It is this realization that no one, absolutely no one, is exempt from suspicion in an Agatha Christie novel that makes reading the finest ones such a delight. Here she will kill off all the characters, there she will make virtually everyone the murderer, somewhere else the crime will be committed by—no, surely not by him? But how could she possibly justify that? Well, she does.

Her puzzles endure to delight and surprise readers towards the end of the twentieth century just as much as they did in the twenties because they are not mechanical but concerned with human character. The locked-room mysteries beloved of John Dickson Carr are of no great interest to Agatha

Christie, nor are the fiendish devices, the evaporating ice darts or any of the other paraphernalia used by some of the earlier crime writers. Her tricks are sometimes verbal, sometimes visual. If you listen carefully and watch her all the time, you *may* catch Mrs Christie, but it is highly unlikely that you will. The solution which she has somehow persuaded you quite early in the narrative is *not* the correct one very frequently *is*—but not invariably.

Mrs Christie is at her best throughout *The Murder of Roger Ackroyd*. The occasional Christie carelessness is there, as when she tells us that Ackroyd is nearly fifty years of age, and a paragraph or two later it becomes clear that he could not have been older than forty-three. And Poirot's years in England have caused his command of French to deteriorate. He says 'Je ne pense pas' when he clearly means 'Je crois que non', and in any case is perfectly capable of saying 'I think not' in English. But these are minor quibbles. In Dr Sheppard and his sister Mrs Christie has created a pair of highly engaging characters, and her description of Caroline Sheppard, tempted to gossip, but wavering for a second or two 'much as a roulette ball might coyly hover between two numbers', is especially felicitous.

You can usually expect a little music in her books and, at least in the early Christies, a little anti-semitism. Both are to be found in *Roger Ackroyd*. Oddly, it is the unmusical Major Blunt who provides the two references to opera when he talks of 'the johnny who sold his soul to the devil' and mentions that 'there's an opera about it', and later reveals his knowledge that Mélisande is someone in an opera. Agatha Christie probably saw both *Faust* and *Pelléas et Mélisande* during her period at finishing school in Paris, but you would not have expected Major Blunt to know Debussy's opera though he might just have been aware of the more popular *Faust* of Gounod. Blunt, incidentally, is a name Mrs Christie seems to have been fond of using. Three more Blunts, one of them an Admiral, will turn up in later works.

The mandatory anti-semitic reference occurs when one of the characters receives demands from debt collectors (Scotch [sic] gentlemen named McPherson and MacDonald), and Dr Sheppard comments: 'They are usually Scotch gentlemen, but I suspect a Semitic strain in their ancestry.'

Two years after its publication, *The Murder of Roger Ackroyd* was adapted for the stage by Michael Morton. Mrs Christie much disliked Morton's first suggestion which was to take about twenty years off Poirot's age, call him Beau Poirot, and have lots of girls in love with him. With the support of Gerald Du Maurier who produced the play, she persuaded the adaptor not to change the character and personality of Poirot, but agreed to allow Caroline Sheppard to be turned into a young and attractive girl, in order to supply Poirot with romantic interest. Mrs Christie's agreement was reluctant. She resented the removal of the spinster Caroline, for she liked the role played by this character in the life of the village, and she liked the idea of that village life being reflected through Dr Sheppard and his sister. In the play, Poirot confesses to Dr Sheppard that he loves Caryl, as she is now called, and although at the end the great detective announces his intention to leave 'for my own country', the final moments suggest that he may, one day, come back for Caryl:

> POIROT (taking both her hands and kissing them): *Un de ces jours . . .*
> CARYL: What do you mean?
> POIROT: Perhaps one day . . .
>   (Caryl goes out slowly. Poirot turns back to table, takes rose out of specimen glass which is on table, kisses it, and puts it in his button-hole, looking off towards the garden where Caryl has gone out.)
> *The curtain falls.*

The play, which was called *Alibi*, opened on 15 May 1928, at the Prince of Wales Theatre in the West End of London, with the twenty-nine-year-old Charles Laughton as Hercule Poirot, J.H. Roberts as Dr Sheppard, Basil Loder as Major Blunt, Henry Daniell (who went to Hollywood the following year to play suave villains in countless American films) as Parker, the butler, Lady Tree as Mrs Ackroyd, Jane Welsh as her daughter Flora, Cyril Nash as Ralph Paton, Henry Forbes Robertson as Geoffrey Raymond, Iris Noel as Ursula Bourne, and Gillian Lind as Caryl Sheppard. *The Sketch* said that Laughton 'admirably impersonated' Poirot, and Mrs Christie thought he was a good actor but 'entirely unlike Hercule Poirot'. The play was a commercial success, running for 250 performances in London before being taken up elsewhere and eventually by amateur dramatic societies with whom it is still highly popular.

In 1931, the play became a film, still with the title of *Alibi*. Produced by Julius Hagen, who had already made an Agatha Christie movie in 1928, and directed by Leslie Hiscott, *Alibi* was filmed at the Twickenham studios near London, with Austin Trevor who was even less like Hercule Poirot than Laughton had been, and who made no attempt at a characterization, but played the role 'straight'. Others in the cast were Franklin Dyall, Elizabeth Allan, Clare Greet and Milton Rosmer. (Max Mallowan in his autobiography, *Malloman's Memoirs*, wrongly identifies the actor who played Poirot in this film as Francis Sullivan, who played Poirot twice on the stage, but who was not in either the film or the stage version of *Alibi*.)

Retitled *The Fatal Alibi*, the play was staged in New York on 28 February 1932, with Charles Laughton directing and also playing Poirot. It closed after twenty-four performances.

The first of Agatha Christie's books to be produced in Great Britain by Collins and in America by Dodd, Mead & Co who had bought John Lane and Co, *The Murder of Roger Ackroyd* was published in the spring of 1926. Seven months later, on Friday, 3 December, Mrs Christie disappeared in mysterious circumstances worthy of one of her crime novels.

The year 1926 had been far from a happy one for Agatha Christie. It began well enough with a brief holiday in Corsica with her sister, during which she worked on *The Mystery of the Blue Train*, but shortly after the sisters arrived home they learned that their mother was ill and some months later she found herself also having to cope with the realization that her marriage to Archie Christie had badly deteriorated. For some time Colonel Christie had seemed to be more interested in golf than in his wife, and now Agatha discovered that she had a more serious rival for her husband's affections, a young woman called Nancy Neele who lived at Godalming in Surrey and who was also an acquaintance of hers. Archie confessed that he was in love with Miss Neele and wanted to marry her. He asked Agatha to divorce him.

On the morning of Friday, 3 December 1926, after a quarrel with his wife, Colonel Christie packed his bags and left home to spend the weekend with Miss Neele in Godalming. That evening, leaving her daughter Rosalind asleep in the house, Mrs Christie drove off in her car. She left two letters, one addressed to Archie, and one requesting her secretary to cancel her appointments as she was going to Yorkshire. According to the daughter of the then Deputy Chief Constable of Surrey, she posted a letter to the Deputy Chief Constable, in which she said she feared for her life, and appealed for his help. Her car was found next morning by George Best, a fifteen-year-old gypsy lad. It had been abandoned on the embankment at the side of the road at a popular 'beauty spot' called Newlands Corner, near a lake known as the Silent Pool. The bodywork of the car was covered in frost, and the lights were still on. Inside the car the police found a fur coat, and a small case which had burst open and which contained three dresses, two pairs of shoes and an expired driving licence in the name of Mrs Agatha Christie.

For the next few days the newspapers were full of stories about the well-known mystery writer's disappearance, with huge banner headlines announcing new so-called developments, interviews with and comments by several people, and speculation by many more. Suicide was not ruled out, nor was murder.

On 7 December, the *Daily News* offered '£100 reward to the first person furnishing us with information leading to the whereabouts, if alive, of Mrs Christie'. The Deputy Chief Constable of Surrey said, in the best tradition of the detective novel: 'I have handled many important cases during my career, but this is the most baffling mystery ever set me for solution.' Also in the best tradition of crime fiction, suspicion centred for a time upon the husband of the missing woman.

By the following weekend, hundreds of policemen and thousands of members of the general public had joined in the search for Agatha Christie. The Silent Pool was dredged with special machinery, light aircraft scoured the countryside from above, and packs of airdales and bloodhounds went over the ground more closely. Police from four counties, Surrey, Essex, Berkshire and Kent, were brought in. As in an Agatha Christie murder mystery, a number of clues were found, only to be discarded as red herrings: a local chemist said that Mrs Christie had often discussed with him methods of committing suicide; a woman claimed that she had seen someone, whom she identified from photographs as Mrs Christie, wandering about, dazed; and two other people remembered that a woman answering to her description, her clothes covered in frost, had asked them the way to Petersfield, a town in Hampshire. The police guarded Colonel Christie's house, monitored his phone calls, and followed him to his office. Christie told a city colleague, 'They think I've murdered my wife.'

The weekend after her disappearance, in answer to an appeal from the police fifteen thousand volunteers searched the Downs. On the Saturday afternoon, three thousand of their cars were parked on Merrow Downs, and they set off in groups of thirty with a police officer in charge of each group. The *Daily Mail* played its part by publishing an article by the famous thriller writer, Edgar Wallace, in which he expounded his theory of Mrs Christie's disappearance. He did not suspect foul play, but considered it

> a typical case of 'mental reprisal' on somebody who has hurt her. To put it vulgarly her first intention seems to have been to 'spite' an unknown person who would be distressed by her disappearance.
>
> That she did not contemplate suicide seems evident from the fact that she deliberately created an atmosphere of suicide by abandonment of her car.
>
> Loss of memory, that is to say mental confusion, might easily have followed but a person so afflicted could not possibly escape notice . . . If Agatha Christie is not dead of shock and exposure within a limited radius of the place

where her car was found, she must be alive and in full possession of her faculties, probably in London. It is impossible to
lose your memory and find your way to a determined desti-
nation.

Edgar Wallace's theory was perfectly tenable, and indeed may well
have been correct. It was certainly quite proper for him to have suggested
it, but perhaps unwise of the chief suspect, Colonel Christie, to put forward
the same idea to the *Daily News:* 'My wife said to me, some time ago, that
she could disappear at will and would defy anyone to find her. This shows
that the possibility of engineering her disappearance was running through
her mind.'

During the week in which Agatha Christie remained missing, the
banjo player in the band at the Hydropathic Hotel at Harrogate, in those
days an elegant spa resort in Yorkshire, informed the Harrogate police of
his suspicion that the Mrs Neele who had been staying at the hotel since
the previous Saturday was, in fact, Mrs Christie. The police stationed a
detective in the hotel for two days to keep an eye on Mrs Neele, and the
manager of the hotel (which is now called the Old Swan Hotel) made a
statement to the police about Mrs Neele:

> She arrived by taxi on Saturday morning with only a small
> suitcase and asked for a bedroom on *en pension* terms and
> was given a good room on the first floor with hot and cold
> water.
>   I did not see her myself but I believe that the price
> quoted to her was seven guineas a week. She accepted this
> without hesitation. Indeed, from the first day she has been
> here she seems to have as much money as she wants. From
> the first her life in the Hydro has been exactly similar to
> that of our other guests. She takes her meals in the dining-
> room and only once or twice has had breakfast in bed. She
> is a very agreeable guest.

When the story that a Mrs Neele at the Hydro Hotel in Harrogate
might well be Agatha Christie was leaked to the press, several newspapers
sent reporters to Harrogate, and the *Daily Mail* sent a special train with a
team of reporters and photographers. It was, however, a *Daily News*
reporter, the twenty-year-old Ritchie Calder (the late Baron Ritchie-
Calder) who walked up to Mrs Neele in the lounge of the hotel and
addressed her as Mrs Christie. 'Mrs Neele' admitted to him that she was

Mrs Christie, but, when asked how she had got to Harrogate, said she did not know as she was suffering from amnesia. She then left Calder abruptly, went up to her room and stayed there for the remainder of the afternoon.

On Tuesday, 14 December, the London *Evening Standard* published the news that Agatha Christie had been found. *The Daily News* sent Mrs Christie a telegram, which they also published: 'In view widespread criticism your disappearance strongly urge desirability authentic explanation from yourself to thousands of public who joined in costly search and cannot understand your loss of memory theory.'

No 'authentic explanation' was ever vouchsafed by Agatha Christie. She had registered at the Hydro Hotel as Mrs Teresa Neele, and had let it be known to fellow guests that she was a visitor from Cape Town. On the evening of the day she arrived, Saturday, 14 December, there was a dance at the hotel, and when the band played 'Yes, We Have No Bananas', Mrs Neele got up and danced the Charleston. She spent her week at Harrogate shopping ('she was constantly buying new clothes,' Miss Corbett, the hotel pianist, told the police), taking tea in a local tea shop, and going on long walks. In the evening she played billiards at the Hydro, and on more than one occasion was prevailed upon to sing in her small but sweet soprano, accompanying herself at the piano. Once in the middle of a sentimental song, she faltered and seemed close to tears, but this was attributed to the fact that 'Mrs Neele' was recovering from the loss of a child in South Africa. During the week she posted an announcement to *The Times*, which appeared in the newspaper's personal column on Saturday, 11 December: 'Friends and relatives of Teresa Neele, late of South Africa, please communicate—Write Box R 702, *The Times*, EC4'.

When he accosted her at the hotel, the young journalist Ritchie Calder thought that 'amnesia', which Mrs Christie flung glibly at him, 'was much too clinical a word for someone supposedly surprised into conversation, and if, as her doctor later suggested, she had an "identity crisis", well, by golly, there was no "Teresa Neele" lurking in the self-possessed woman I met.'

Archie Christie arrived in Harrogate at 6.45 p.m. on Tuesday, 14 December, and identified his wife as she walked through the lounge of the hotel wearing an orchid pink dinner gown. She appeared unembarrassed as he walked up to her, merely turning to a group of fellow guests and saying, 'Fancy, my brother has just arrived'. One of the guests who watched the reunion said later that the Christies then sat down in front of the fire in the lounge, but several chairs apart from each other as though they had been quarrelling. They stayed overnight, not in Mrs Neele's room but in a suite. Colonel Christie made an announcement to the press:

> There is no question about the identity. It is my wife. She has
> suffered from the most complete loss of memory and I do not
> think she knows who she is. She does not know me and she
> does not know where she is. I am hoping that the rest and
> quiet will restore her. I am hoping to take her to London
> tomorrow to see a doctor and specialists.

Two doctors, a neurologist and a general practitioner, issued a statement to
the effect that Mrs Christie was 'suffering from an unquestionable loss of
memory and that for her future welfare she should be spared all anxiety and
excitement.' In other words, ask no questions.

The press accused Mrs Christie of having planned her disappearance
merely to obtain publicity. That was a nonsensical accusation, for she was not
only a shy woman who avoided publicity as much as possible, she was also in
no need of it. But she was certainly not the victim of amnesia. The week before
her disappearance, Agatha Christie had lost a diamond ring at Harrods. She
wrote to the Knightsbridge department store from Harrogate, describing the
ring and asking that, if it were found, it be sent to Mrs Teresa Neele at the
Hydro Hotel. Harrods did, in fact, return Mrs Christie's ring to Mrs Neele.

In 1980 in a magazine called *The Bookseller*, a very elderly journalist
claimed to remember that, in 1926, on the morning after Mrs Christie disappeared, her publisher Sir Godfrey Collins had told him not to talk to anyone
about it, as Mrs Christie was in Harrogate, resting.

The strongest likelihood is that a very unhappy Mrs Archibald
Christie had come close to nervous collapse, and that it was in a condition
of considerable mental turmoil that she, nonetheless deliberately, staged
her disappearance in such a way as to cause the maximum distress to the
man whom she loved and who had caused her such anguish. She probably
hoped that he would think she had killed herself and would suffer remorse.
She may even have hoped that he would be suspected of having murdered
her. Perhaps she thought her disappearance would bring Archie to a realization of how much he needed her. Normal, warmhearted and affectionate
a creature though she was, Mrs Christie was not necessarily more so than
many another who had been driven by extreme mental anguish to commit
actions which seem wildly out of character. Far from disappearing in order
to court publicity, she was so distraught at the collapse of her marriage that
she was driven to a course of extremely neurotic behaviour despite her fear
of publicity. And, her most successful novel having been published seven
months earlier and sold extremely well, she had no need of publicity.

In her autobiography, written in old age, Agatha Christie made no
direct reference to these exciting events of 1926, contenting herself merely

with the observation that after illness came sorrow, despair and heartbreak, and that there was no need to dwell on it. Further clues to the mystery of her behaviour in December 1926 are inextricably embedded in the crypto-auto-biographical novel, *Unfinished Portrait*, which she wrote a few years later.

GILLIAN GILL

Afterward: The Secret of Success

The central facts of Christie's view of the world were her reluctance to give information, particularly about herself, her difficulty in expressing deep emotion, her belief that only through God and after death could one truly know another human person, and her feeling of closeness with the sensual world. The central fact of Christie's writing is that she has attracted millions of devoted fans all over the world and continues to do so through films and television as well as books and plays. What makes the created world of this eccentric and reclusive woman so popular?

Christie's fiction is unabashedly mass-market art, and on the surface the aim of mass-market art seems to be as simple as its techniques are sophisticated—to make money for the producer by giving the target audience what it wants. Yet even as this mass-market product aggressively defines itself as anti-intellectual and devoid of content, it attains a paradoxical importance as ideology. On a fantasy level, it is able to express, maintain, subvert, or advance powerful social and psychic movements. Structured into the plot of a novel, the images of a film, or the layout of an advertisement, is an expression of raw emotions, memories, and drives that tend to lose their motivating energy when they emerge into consciousness. It is popular art's ability to tap into the collective unconscious while bypassing the reason that accounts for the cultural significance of such apparently trivial subgenres as the harlequin or gothic

From *Agatha Christie: The Woman and Her Mysteries* by Gillian Gill. © 1990 by The Free Press.

romance, cowboy books, mystery novels, spy fiction, and, in the visual field, television soap operas, private-eye series, horror movies, and commercials.

Sometimes characters or sets of characters created in popular literature transcend the texts which generate them and take on the quality of a modern myth. Crusoe and Friday, Dracula and his brides, Frankenstein and his monster, Tarzan and Jane, Holmes and Watson and Moriarty, Svengali and Trilby, the Phantom of the Opera and Christine Daaé—are all figures from popular art that crystallize a web of relations of such cultural resonance as to defy normal boundaries of time and place. Hercule Poirot and Miss Marple, those vigilant defenders of society against the evil ever within it, possess this mythic energy, which has little do with conventional portrayal of realistic or "rounded" characters. Paradoxically for a writer so overtly committed to the superiority of the reason and the ego as epitomized by Poirot's "little grey cells," Christie's essential appeal as a writer is perhaps to the reader's unconscious.

That the unconscious is at work in Christie's fiction can be seen in the mirroring devotion of the writer to her writing and of the public to her work. Painstakingly, reliably, year after year, Agatha Christie built up a fictional world which three generations of men and women have turned to in search of that apparently simple commodity, "mere" entertainment. The progress of the writer herself through fifty-five years of writing and some eighty-six completed volumes indicates an authorial compulsiveness that goes beyond the simply financial motivations Christie avows. Had Christie really written her books for the practical and contingent reasons she admits to in her autobiography, had writing been as tiresome and nerve-wracking a job as she likes to tell us, she would surely not have continued writing until the very end of her life. After 1938, for example, when Max's career had taken off, Rosalind was grown up, Greenway was bought, and royalites from some thirty successful titles were rolling in, Christie had no practical need to keep writing. Dorothy L. Sayers at essentially this stage in her life did decide to write no more detective stories. Sayers felt she would be happier doing something else and had already published enough to keep her in comfort for the rest of her days. And just as Christie compulsively produced book after book, in good times and bad, whether she needed the money or not, so the public has responded to Christie's books, buying them in larger and larger numbers, regardless of "quality," apparently insatiable for plays and films based on her writing. Such compulsiveness in an international public over many decades demands more complex explanations than that people like a good yarn, or a neat puzzle.

Agatha Christie was herself a devoted reader of detective fiction. She remembers in her autobiography how fascinated she was at age eight when

Madge read her *The Leavenworth Case*, and she refers to herself and Madge as connoisseurs of the detective story. Thus, when she came to write mystery fiction, Christie had not only expert knowledge but also a fan's intuitive understanding of the genre and the hold it had over the public. However, this empathy between Christie and her potential audience was built upon a rare and much more fundamental correlation between writer and target reader.

The public for the various subgenres of popular literature divides sharply into subgroups that find pleasure in subtle variations on an established formula. The detective-story readers, in contrast with devotees of romance or adventure, see themselves as intelligent realists, not romantic escapists, and they have a strong preference that message and meaning be presented implicitly through clues laid by an authorial voice that is trustworthy but never intrusive. This readership preference coincided to an almost unique extent with the psychic requirements of Agatha Christie. Agatha Miller had, from childhood, a quite extraordinary problem in speaking her inner world or giving even trivial information about what she thought and knew. This intense reserve was reinforced by the failure of her first marriage. In later life, Christie's exceptional success and happiness depended upon her rare freedom to structure a private and public realm in which she was not required to explain herself, even to friends, or to make speeches for the public. Consciously, her novels are an attempt not to reveal but to mask the self, yet even as she succeeds in eliminating personal opinions and autobiographical information, Christie thereby gives free rein to her unconscious. Hers is a fictional world in which the author is hidden, and which fixes readers' minds upon the analysis of emotionally neutral elements, such as cigarette butts and railway timetables, while sweeping their fantasies along on an effortless, unthinking race to the denouement.

It is no accident, then that Christie never lost her childhood fascination with fairy stories—"fairy stories were her passion. Stories of real-life children did not much interest her," writes Christie of her alter ego Celia in *Unfinished Portrait*—and that fairy-tale themes ring out so insistently in her work. *Ten Little Indians; One, Two, Buckle My Shoe; Crooked House; Hickory Dickory Dock; Five Little Pigs; A Pocket Full of Rye; Three Blind Mice; Cat Among the Pigeons*—how many of Agatha Christie's titles recall the world of childhood fairy tales, the world of Mother Goose and the Brothers Grimm? The fairy-tale world is today recognized as a vital expression of the collective unconscious, revealing a special kind of archetypal truth. Christie's writing has the sparseness, the directness, the narrative pace, and the universal appeal of the fairy story, and it is perhaps as modern fairy stories for grown-up children that Christie's novels succeed.

"I don't know anything about him," says the enigmatic Isabella of her lover John Gabriel just before her death. A scene later in *The Rose and the Yew Tree*, Teresa, while assuring Hugh Norreys that he is not responsible for Isabella's death, says to him, "You loved her enough to leave her alone." These two bald sentences are emblematic of Agatha Christie's strange and yet compelling vision of life. A woman of strong views, a woman convinced that there are eternal values and verities, Christie was yet singularly free of evangelical zeal and didactic purpose. If she had a message, it was that each person should and must make choices for himself or herself and should impinge as little as possible upon the choices of others. In the words of Thomas à Kempis, "You are not required to answer for others but you will have to give an account of your own life." Humility, tolerance, and acceptance are for Christie the essential virtues. She reserved her anger and condemnation not for the sinners of the flesh, but for those who see themselves as more than other men, who use their talent to bind others to their will and their strength to kill and maim.

Physical ardor, a passionate response to the whole world of the senses—to nature, to human beauty, to music, art, and literature, to good food—combined in Agatha Christie with a mental coolness to create a fictional world whose very reserve and refusal of allure constitute its greatest attraction. Agatha Christie makes no claim to know her readers, merely to respect and enjoy us. She loves us enough to leave us alone, and we love her for it.

ANNE HART

The Curtain Rises

> "My name," said Poirot, contriving as usual to make the simple statement sound like the curtain of the first act of a play, "my name is Hercule Poirot."
> —*The Labors of Hercules*

That benevolent despot, Hercule Poirot, who to this day keeps a firm grasp on the affection of countless subjects , made his debut as a fully formed foreign eccentric on page thirty-four of his creator's first book, *The Mysterious Affair at Styles*. On page thirty-five Cynthia Murdoch of Styles court made a pioneer English attempt to describe him: "He's a dear little man," she said.

Her remark was to stand the test of time, wonderfully well, though not everyone who was to meet Poirot over the next six decades—especially not those attempting to cover up crimes—would agree with her. "You unutterable little jackanapes of a foreigner!" more than one was to cry, purple with rage. Poirot himself would have been annoyed if he had heard Cynthia's remark. "My name is Hercule Poirot," he was apt to say to those not appropriately impressed, "and I am probably the greatest detective in the world."

From *The Life and Times of Hercule Poirot*. © 1990 by G. P. Putnam's Sons.

A number of Christie scholars have debated his origins. The most important clues, of course, have been provided by Agatha Christie herself. In 1916, in her twenty-sixth year, she set herself the task of writing a detective novel:

> Who could I have as a detective? I reviewed such detectives as I had met and admired in books. There was Sherlock Holmes, the one and only—I should never be able to emulate *him*. There was Arsene Lupin—was he a criminal or a detective? Anyway, not my kind. There was the young journalist Rouletabille in *The Mystery of the Yellow Room*—that was the *sort* of person whom I would like to invent . . . then I remembered our Belgian refugees. We had quite a colony of refugees living in the parish of Tor . . . Why not make my detective a Belgian? I thought. There were all types of refugees. How about a refugee police officer? A retired police officer. Not too young a one . . .
>
> Anyway, I settled on a Belgian detective. I allowed him slowly to grow into his part. He should have been an inspector, so that he would have certain knowledge of crime. He would be meticulous, very tidy . . . always arranging things, liking things in pairs, liking things square instead of round. And he should be very brainy—he should have little gray cells of the mind—that was a good phrase: I must remember that—yes, he would have little gray cells.

Other possible predecessors and contemporaries have been suggested: G. K. Chesterton's Hercule Flambeau, Robert Barr's Eugène Valmont, A. E. W. Mason's Inspector Hanaud, Marie Belloc Lowndes' Hercules Popeau, and inevitably—despite Agatha Christie's disclaimer—Sherlock Holmes.

Like Holmes, Poirot was vain, brilliant, and a bachelor; like Holmes he possessed, in Arthur Hastings, a faithful Watson; and, as readers will discover, there occur from time to time in the Poirot canon situations and frames of mind distinctly Holmesian. "Ah, well," as Poirot himself said complacently in *Cards on the Table*, "I am not above stealing the tricks of others." *He* knew perfectly well who he was. He was the one and only, the unique Hercule Poirot. If *he* had been asked about origins, I imagine him stroking his moustaches, his eyes as green as a cat's. "Once upon a time," he might have replied, with an imperious wave of his hand, "there was born in the kingdom of Belgium a baby with an egg-shaped head. . . ."

The kingdom of Belgium was—and still is—a neat, cautious, Catholic country that knows what it's about. Family businesses flourish. Education and the arts are taken seriously and so is food. Its restaurants are well known to gourmets and its pastry chefs are famous.

Its capital, Brussels—the city where Poirot was probably born and certainly flourished for many years—possesses one of the most beautiful and sociable squares in Europe, the Grand' Place. Here, high atop the magnificent Hôtel de Ville, a gilded figure of St. Michael watches over the city. It is perfectly possible that, once upon a time, St. Michael watched a procession of Poirots taking a new baby to church to be christened.

When was Hercule Poirot born? In what he himself would have called "supreme exercises of imagination," a number of serious attempts have been made to pinpoint one improbable year or another. Usually these calculations depend on a remark of Poirot's in *Three Act Tragedy* that he was "due" to retire from the Belgian Police Force at the time of the outbreak of the First World War. Making an undocumented guess at a retirement age of sixty to sixty-five years, the conclusion has then been reached that he was born between 1849 and 1854.

Tempting as it is to reconstruct a chronological Poirot in this matter of age—particularly as he was still flourishing in the early 1970's—I suspect that Agatha Christie, and Poirot himself, would have been amused by all this arithmetic. In context, Poirot seems to be man in his late fifties or early sixties when he arrives in England, and somewhere in his mid-eighties in *Curtain*, his last case. That close to sixty years of elegant aging elapsed between, with never a diminution of his gray cells, was a *tour de force* for his adroit creator and one of Poirot's great charms. "Men have as many years as they feel," says an Italian proverb. In this matter of years, and of his age at any particular time, Poirot was always extremely—and wisely—reticent.

In *The Labors of Hercules* Dr. Burton, a fellow of All Souls College, ruminated on Hercule Poirot's first name. "Hardly a *Christian* name," he pointed out. "Definitely pagan. But why? That's what I want to know. Father's fancy? Mother's whim?" Whether moved by fancy or whim, the Poirots showed no timidity. In an inspired moment they delved into Greek mythology and named their son for Hercules the strong, the mightiest of the ancient heroes. Poirot himself loved his name; it was to prove a glorious compensation for his diminutive size. "It is the name of one of the great ones of this world," he boasted in *The Mystery of the Blue Train*.

All of his life Poirot preferred privacy and was particularly unforthcoming about his earlier (and long) life in Belgium. References to his past are rare, but in *Three Act Tragedy* we are permitted an insight into his childhood: "See you, as a boy I was poor. There were many of us. We had to get on in the world." One glimpses the Poirots again, hard-working and close-knit, in his lifelong devotion to The Family. "I am very strong on the family life, as you know," he declared to Hastings on one occasion, and "Family strength is a marvelous thing," he said on another.

Papa Poirot is scarcely mentioned. All evidence suggests that the mother was the strong one in this family. "Madam, we, in our country, have a great tenderness, a great respect for the mother. The *mère de famille*, she is everything!" was how he introduced himself to a matron in "The King of Clubs," and "I comprehend the mother's heart. No one comprehends it better than I, Hercule Poirot," he told the Dowager Duchess of Merton in *Lord Edgware Dies*. Throughout his life he was to stand in awe of mothers. "Mothers, Madame, are particularly ruthless when their children are in danger," he said to a somewhat enigmatic one in *Death on the Nile*. Perhaps Madame Poirot had cause to be formidable? One imagines her determined and orderly, keeping strict accounts, supervising lessons, fighting against considerable odds to bring her children up to be good little *bourgeois*, and insisting, in their small quarters, that everyone have good manners and be very neat. Is it Madame Poirot we are seeing, shepherding her large flock to church, in Poirot's recollection of how women looked in his youth? " . . . a coiffure high and rigid—so—and the hat attached with many hatpins—*là—là—là et là.*"

But life was not all obedience and hard work. Madame Poirot's children had some good times as well. "*Les Feux d'Artifices*, the Party, the Games with balls," recalled Poirot in *Peril at End House*. Little Hercule must have been especially enthralled with "the conjuror, the man who deceives the eye, however carefully it watches." And they all must have had a splendid time at the Ommegang, the great holiday in July when the Grand' Place is thronged with merrymakers. Like most Europeans, however, Poirot regarded childhood as not a particularly desirable state, but as something to be got over with as quickly as possible. In *Mrs. McGinty's Dead*, listening to Superintendent Spence dwell in nostalgic detail on the pleasure of childhood:

> Poirot waited politely. This was one of the moments when,
> even after half a lifetime in the country, he found the English
> incomprehensible. He himself had played at *Cache Cache* in
> this childhood, but he felt no desire to talk about it or even
> think about it.

What of his brothers and sisters? "There were many of us," he told Mr. Satterthwaite, but there is a mention of only one of them in all the Poirot literature, and it is a mention that is quickly erased. In the original version of "the Chocolate Box," a short story that reveals his earlier days in Belgium, Poirot says:

"I was informed that young lady was demanding me. Thinking that it was, perhaps, my little sister Yvonne, I prayed my landlady to make her mount."

Later versions of this story omit this reference to Yvonne, but it does provide an affectionate glimpse of Poirot as an older brother, a glimpse reflected in an avuncular way a generation later in *Cards on the Table* when Poirot says to a young woman:

"It is, you understand, that Christmas is coming on. I have to buy presents for many nieces and grand-nieces."

One has to be a bit wary about this mention of nieces and grand-nieces, however, as Poirot, who practically never mentioned his real family, was apt to invent imaginary relatives to suit his purposes. The most outrageous example of this is the appearance among the *dramatis personae* of *The Big Four* of a twin brother, Achille. When first told of this hitherto unsuspected twin, Hastings was understandably surprised. "'What does he do?'" he demanded, "putting aside a half-formed wonder as to the character and disposition of the late Madame Poirot, and her classical taste in Christian names." Replied Poirot, smoothly:

"He does nothing. He is, as I tell, of a singularly indolent disposition. But his abilities are hardly less than my own—which is saying a great deal."
"Is he like you to look at?"
"Not unlike. But not nearly so handsome. And wears no moustaches."

In *The Murder of Roger Ackroyd* Poirot invented a nephew to extract information from that indomitable purveyor of village news, Miss Caroline Sheppard. "I never knew that Poirot had an imbecile nephew?" said her brother, Dr. Sheppard.

"Didn't you? Oh, he told me all about it. Poor lad. It's a great grief to all the family. They've kept him at home so far, but it's getting to such a pitch that they're afraid he'll have to go to some kind of institution."
"I suppose you know pretty well everything there is to know about Poirot's family by this time," I said, exasperated.
"Pretty well," said Caroline complacently. "It's a great

relief to people to be able to tell all their troubles to some one."

In *Dumb Witness*, to Hastings' amusement, Poirot produced three more unfortunate relatives: an invalid uncle, a cousin with jaundice, and an ailing but belligerent mother:

> This time he had an aged mother for whom he was anxious to find a sympathetic hospital nurse.
>
> "You comprehend—I am going to speak to you quite frankly. My mother, she is difficult. We have had some excellent nurses, young women, fully competent, but the very fact that they are young has been against them. My mother dislikes young women, she insults them, she is rude and fractious, she fights against open windows and modern hygiene. It is very difficult."

There may, of course, have been germs of truth in some of these confidences, but before leaving the subject of Poirot's relatives, both real and imaginary, we can be sure that he once had a grandfather who possessed "a large turnip of a watch" (Hastings called it "a large grotesque turnip of a watch") and that Poirot fell heir to it. "Take my watch in your hand—with care," he once instructed. "It is a family heirloom!"

As a young child, Poirot, a good little Catholic, was educated by nuns. There is an evocative scene in "The Apples of the Hesperides" when, working on a case in Ireland, he heard the tolling of a convent bell. At once he was transported back in time: "He understood that bell. It was a sound he had been familiar with from early youth." He may have heard it with mixed feelings. In *Five Little Pigs* there is a clue that his convent school had its share of dragons. In meeting "the shrewd, penetrating glance" of a retired governess, Poirot "Once again felt the years falling away and himself a meek and apprehensive little boy."

As to his later education—and despite Dr. Burton's suspicions that he was never properly taught the classics—Poirot appears to have undergone a thorough and conventional schooling including the study of English, German and Italian in addition, of course, to the two languages of Belgium, French and Flemish. "Alas, there is no proper education nowadays," he lamented in *After the Funeral*. "Apparently one learns nothing but economics—and how to set Intelligence Tests!"

It is not easy to imagine Poirot as a youth, his moustache in mere infancy, but bits and pieces emerge in the kindness he later showed to injudicious and awkward young men. "I cannot overcome my shyness. I say always the wrong thing. I upset water jugs," confessed one of them in *Murder in Mesopotamia*. "'We all do these things when we are young,' said Poirot, smiling. 'The poise, the *savoir faire*, it comes later,'" and "it is the time for follies, when one is young," he said encouragingly to another in "The Adventure of the Christmas Pudding."

An endearing glimpse of Poirot himself as a youth is provided in *Evil Under the Sun:*

> "When I was young (and that, Mademoiselle, is indeed a long time ago) there was a game entitled '*If not yourself, who would you be?*' One wrote the answer in young ladies' albums. They had gold edges and were bound in blue leather."

From an early age Poirot knew exactly who he would be:

> "To most of us the test comes early in life. A man is confronted quite soon with the necessity to stand on his own feet, to face dangers and difficulties and to take his own line of dealing with them."

And here we have it, the surprising lure to this tidy and diminutive young man of a life of dangers and difficulties. "I entered the police force," he told Mr. Satterthwaite.

In Poirot's day, Belgium claimed to have an almost perfect statute book and was considered one of the least policed countries in Europe, so law abiding were her citizens. Nevertheless, Poirot—who quickly became attached to the judicial police whose duties were to investigate crimes and apprehend offenders—had at least one combative moment. A reminiscence in *Curtain* recalls him in a startling role—Poirot, the Sharpshooter:

> "As a young man in the Belgian police force I shot down a desperate criminal who sat on a roof and fired at people below."

In a few laconic sentences, Poirot, many years later, summed up perhaps forty to forty-five years he spent with the Belgian police:

> "I worked hard. Slowly I rose in that force. I began to make a name for myself. I made a name for myself. I began to acquire an international reputation."

Poirot's career was brilliant. In time he became head of the force. As Hastings described him in *The Mysterious Affair at Styles:*

> . . . this quaint dandified little man . . . had been in his time one of the most celebrated members of the Belgian police. As a detective, his flair had been extraordinary, and he had achieved triumphs by unraveling some of the most baffling cases of the day.

In his English life Poirot occasionally spoke of these Belgian days, and when he did it was almost always of the one case in which he had been utterly fooled.

This dreadful experience was recounted one stormy night as Poirot and Hastings traded confidences before the fire ("Outside, the wind howled malevolently, and the rain beat against the windows in great gusts"). "You ask me if I have ever made the complete ass of myself, as you say over here?" said Poirot, and there followed the story of "The Chocolate Box," a case of a political murder in Brussels in which, outfoxed by a most unlikely killer, he had completely misread the evidence and nearly arrested the wrong person. "*Sapristi!* It does not bear thinking of!" he cried (but what a consolation for Hastings, one can't help thinking).

Another case Poirot recalled from time to time—"one of my early successes"—was the affair of the soap manufacture of Liège, a man of porcine appearance who was found guilty of poisoning his wife in order to marry his secretary. In "The Nemean Lion," while gazing upon "the swelling jowl, the small pig eyes, the bulbous nose, and the close-lipped mouth" of his client, Sir Joseph Hoggin, "a memory stirred dimly. A long time ago . . . in Belgium . . . something, surely, to do with *soap* . . ." On a hunch that his client was up to no good, Poirot immediately recounted the story of The Soap-maker of Liège to Sir Joseph, who went quite pale. Before long his wife, Lady Hoggin, was saying to her husband: "Funny, this tonic tastes quite different. It hasn't got that bitter taste any more. I wonder why?" Poirot was especially proud of this case. "Prevention, always, is better than cure," he said of it in *Hickory Dickory Dock.*

Two collaborations with the British police in these earlier days (Poirot spoke a tolerable, if mannered, English) were to have important consequences, as it was through them that he met the ebullient Inspector Jimmy Japp of Scotland Yard. In 1916, in *The Mysterious Affair at Styles*—Poirot's first case as a private detective in England—he encountered Japp again:

> "I fear you do not remember me, Inspector Japp."

"Why, if it isn't Mr. Poirot!" cried the Inspector. He
turned to the other man. "You've heard me speak of Mr.
Poirot? It was in 1904 he and I worked together—the Abercrombie forgery case—you remember, he was run down in
Brussels. Ah, those were great days, moosier. Then, do you
remember 'Baron' Altara? There was a pretty rogue for you!
He eluded the clutches of half the police in Europe. But we
nailed him in Antwerp—thanks to Mr. Poirot here."

After this, Japp took Poirot under his wing—or was it the other way
around? No matter, in England their guarded friendship would flourish for
years.

In the long run, the most significant link Poirot forged with England
in his Belgian days was the assistance he gave to Arthur Hastings, a young
employee of Lloyd's. The nature of the business that brought Hastings from
London to Brussels is not recorded, but through it he met Poirot and fell
hopelessly under his spell. Hastings was ripe for this. "Well, I've always had
a secret hankering to be a detective!" he confessed to a new friend in *The
Mysterious Affair at Styles.*

"The real thing—Scotland Yard? Or Sherlock
Holmes?"
"Oh, Sherlock Holmes by all means. But really, seri-
ously, I am awfully drawn to it."

Hastings came back from Belgium inspired and reciting at every
opportunity "the various exploits and triumphs of Hercule Poirot." That in
a few years he would be permitted to work under the tutelage of this great
man would have been, at that time, the stuff of his wildest dreams.

As we have seen, Poirot was due to retire in about 1914. Perhaps he
had already begun to plan a quiet new life amidst *"les dunes impeccables"* of
Knocke-sur-mer? In August of 1914, however, catastrophe struck with the
invasion of neutral Belgium by Germany. The Great War had begun.

The years of German occupation were a period of great suffering for
Belgium. Under a German governor, many Belgians who refused to collab-
orate were executed or deported. In defiance workers withdrew their
services, universities voluntarily closed, and newspapers ceased publication.
A British heroine, Edith Cavell, the Matron of the Belgian School of
Nursing, was shot for aiding escaped Allied soldiers. Countless patriots
went underground.

Somewhere in this resistance, we may be sure, was Poirot. As chief of

a police force that declined to cooperate he would have been a prime target
for imprisonment by *les Bosches*—or worse—for under the occupation the
penalty for those in the Belgian intelligence service was death. For almost
two years Poirot dropped from sight. Evidence of his importance to the
resistance surfaced toward the end of the war in the case of "The
Kidnapped Prime Minister," a commission that came from the highest
levels of the British Government. "What made you come to me?" he asked
a delegation from the War Cabinet. "I am unknown, obscure in this great
London of yours." From the reply it is clear that it had been King Albert
himself, the Belgian's monarch in exile, who had suggested his small
compatriot as the one person in England capable of wresting a missing
prime minster from the enemy.

In the spring of 1916 the Germans must have been closing in on
Poirot. Badly wounded, he was smuggled out of Belgium into France. Years
later, in *Murder on the Orient Express*, he reminded a French General of the
debt he owed him:

> "But indeed, do I not remember that once you saved my
> life?" And then the General had made another fitting reply to
> that, disclaiming any merit for that past service; and with
> more mention of France, of Belgium, of glory, of honor and
> of such kindred things they had embraced each other heartily.

From France Poirot came, "a sad and weary refugee to England."

From the outset of the war the English had opened their hearts and
homes to Belgian refugees. "REMEMBER BELGIUM" admonished enlistment
posters, and "*Vivent les braves Belges!*" was the cry, even some seven years
later, of the young people in "The Adventure of the Christmas Pudding."
Hard-working officials toiled to place these bewildered exiles with appropriate benefactors. Where, they must have wondered, should they send this
funny little policeman? Perhaps to Mrs. Ingelthorp?

Emily Ingelthorp, the autocratic mistress of Styles Court in the pretty
Essex village of Styles St. Mary, had already established a colony of six
Belgians in a small cottage called Leastways, not far from the park gates. In
the early summer of 1916, her seventh refugee limped down from a train at
the village station.

"A kind lady gave me hospitality," said Poirot of Mrs. Inglethorp. "We
Belgians will always remember her with gratitude." At Leastways he was
given an upstairs room and there he seems to have spent most of his days
sitting by a window overlooking the village street, smoking an occasional
Russian cigarette, and pondering his fate. "You may speak for yourself,

Hasting," said Poirot in *Curtain*. "For me, my arrival at Styles St. Mary was a sad and painful time. I was a refugee, wounded, exiled from home and country, existing by charity in a foreign land."

What was he to do now, the famous Hercule Poirot, suddenly without aim and far from young? Time must have passed very slowly in this quiet sanctuary "in the midst of green fields and country lanes."

I am sure, as an occasional diversion, that Poirot and his compatriots were hospitably summoned to Styles Court—Styles, as the family called it— to have tea with Mrs. Ingelthorp and her *ménage*. At Mrs. Ingelthorp's side would have been her new husband, her junior by twenty years, the black-bearded Alfred Ingelthorp (the "fortune hunter," her bitter family called him). The refugees would have been introduced as well to Mrs. Ingelthorp's two stepsons from an earlier marriage, John Cavendish, who played at being a country squire, and Lawrence, who published "rotten verses in fancy bind-ings." And they would have met Mary, John Cavendish's stormy-eyed wife, and plucky Cynthia Murdoch, another of Mrs. Ingelthorp's *protégées*.

"You've been entertaining a celebrity unawares," Hastings was to tell them later, and it is interesting to imagine Poirot observing this promising group as he politely sipped a cup of the dreaded English tea. Perhaps, for the first time since coming to England, a gleam of professional interest appeared in those inquiring green eyes?

Chronology

1890 Born Agatha Mary Clarissa Miller on September 15th.

1901 Father, Frederick Alvah Miller, dies.

1910 Christie spends season in Cairo.

1914 Marries Archibald Christie.

1919 Daughter, Rosalind, born.

1920 *The Mysterious Affair at Styles* is published.

1922 *The Secret Adversary* is published.

1923 Finishes British Empire Exhibition Mission. Stops include Canada, Australia, New Zealand, and South Africa.

1926 *The Murder of Roger Ackroyd* is published. Mother, Clara Miller, dies. Christie disappears from society.

1928 Divorces Archibald Christie. Takes an excursion to the Near East. *The Mystery of the Blue Train* is published.

1929   Takes second trip to the Near East. Meets Max Mallowan.

1930   Marries Max Mallowan. Publishes three books: *The Mysterious Mr. Quin, Murder at the Vicarage,* and *Giant's Bread.*

1934   *Murder on the Orient Express* and *Unfinished Portrait* are published.

1935   *Three-Act Tragedy* is published.

1936   *The ABC Murders, Murder in Mesopotamia,* and *Cards on the Table* are published.

1937   Max Mallowan takes part in the excavation of Tell Brak, Syria.

1938   *Appointment with Death* and *Hercule Poirot's Christmas* are published.

1939   *Ten Little Niggers* is published.

1940   *One, Two, Buckle My Shoe* and *Sad Cypress* are published.

1942   Grandson, Matthew Prichard, is born. *The Body in the Library* is published.

1944   Hubert Prichard is killed in action. *Absent in the Spring* and *Towards Zero* are published.

1945   Max Mallowan returns from war. *Death Comes at the End* is published.

1946   *Come, Tell Me How You Live* is published.

1947   *The Labours of Hercules* is published.

1948   *Taken at the Flood* and *Witness for the Prosecution and Other Stories* are published.

1949   Rosalind Anthony Prichard marries Anthony Hicks.

1950   *The Mousetrap and Other Stories* and *A Murder Is Announced* are published.

1952   *The Mousetrap*, the play, and *Witness for the Prosecution*, the play, are produced.
1956   Named Commander of the British Empire.

1958   *Ordeal by Innocence* is published.

1961   *The Pale Horse* is published.

1965   *At Bertram's Hotel* is published.

1967   *Endless Night* is published.

1969   *Hallowe'en Party* is published.

1970   *Passenger to Frankfurt: An Extravaganza* is published.

1971   Named Dame of the British Empire.

1972   *Elephants Can Remember* is published.

1975   *Curtain* is published.

1976   Dies 12, January. *Sleeping Murder* is published posthumously.

1977   *An Autobiography* is published.

Contributors

HAROLD BLOOM is Sterling Professor of the Humanities at Yale University and Henry W. and Albert A. Berg Professor of English at the New York University Graduate School. He is the author of over 20 books, including *Shelley's Mythmaking* (1959), *The Visionary Company* (1961), *Blake's Apocalypse* (1963), *Yeats* (1970), *A Map of Misreading* (1975), *Kabbalah and Criticism* (1975), *Agon: Toward a Theory of Revisionism* (1982), *The American Religion* (1992), *The Western Canon* (1994), and *Omens of Millennium: The Gnosis of Angels, Dreams, and Resurrection* (1996). *The Anxiety of Influence* (1973) sets forth Professor Bloom's provocative theory of the literary relationships between the great writers and their predecessors. His most recent books include *Shakespeare: The Invention of the Human*, a 1998 National Book Award finalist, and *How to Read and Why*, which was published in 2000. In 1999, Professor Bloom received the prestigious American Academy of Arts and Letters Gold Medal for Criticism.

G. C. RAMSEY has been an instructor of English at Worcester Academy in Massachusetts. She has studied Agatha Christie's work in this country and abroad. She is the author of *Agatha Christie: Mistress of Mystery*.

ELIZABETH WALTER has been an editor at Collins Publishers since 1961. She is a distinguished writer of the supernatural. Her works include *Come and Get Me* and *Dead Woman*.

DOROTHY B. HUGHES has been a mystery critic for a quarter of a century, chiefly for the *Los Angeles Times* and the *New York Herald Tribune*.

She is the author of several suspense novels, as well as a biography on Erle Stanley Gardner.

AGATHA CHRISTIE was one of the foremost mystery writers ever. She has published novels, plays, stories, and poetry.

JULIAN SYMONS is the author of a history of crime writing, *Bloody Murder*, as well as several biographies and novels, including *The Colour of Murder*, which won the Crime Writers' Association prize for 1953.

PAM McALLISTER is a lecturer, writer, and the editor of *Reweaving the Web of Life: Feminism and Non-Violence*. She is on the staff of a rape crisis center in Brooklyn.

ROBERT BARNARD is a professor of English Literature at the University of Tromso, Europe's most northerly university. He is the author of many crime novels including *Death of an Old Goat*, *Death on the High C's*, and *Blood Brotherhood*.

CHARLES OSBORNE is the Literature Director of the Arts Council of Great Britain. He is the author of a number of books, including *Kafka*, *The Concert Song Companion*, and *The Complete Operas of Mozart*.

GILLIAN GILL was born in Britain but has spent most of her life as a writer and scholar in the United States. She is the author of *Agatha Christie*, a critical study.

ANNE HART is a librarian at the Memorial University of Newfoundland. She is the author of a number of short stories, poems and plays, as well as the critical volume *The Life and Times of Miss Jane Marple*.

Bibliography

Auden, W. H. "The Guilty Vicarage." *In The Dyer's Hand and Other Essays*. London: Random House, 1962.

Bargainnier, Earl F. *The Gentle Art of Murder: The Detective Fiction of Agatha Christie*. Bowling Green, Ohio: Bowling Green State University Popular Press, 1980.

Barnard, Robert. *A Talent to Deceive: An Appreciation of Agatha Christie*. New York: Dodd, Mead, 1980.

Barnes, Melvyn. *The Best Detective Fiction: A Guide from Godwin to the Present*. Hamden, Conn., and London: Clive Bingley/Linnet Books, 1975.

Barzun, Jacques, and Taylor, W. H. *A Catalogue of Crime*. New York: Harper and Row, 1971.

Bettelheim, Bruno. *The Uses of Enchantment: The Meaning and Importance of Fairy Tales*. New York: Knopf, 1976.

Cassiday, Bruce, ed. *Roots of Detection: The Art of Deduction before Sherlock Holmes*. New York: Frederick Ungar, 1983.

Cawelti, John G. *Adventure, Mystery and Romance: Formula Stories as Art and Popular Culture*. Chicago: University of Chicago Press, 1976.

Champigny, Robert. *What Will Have Happened? A Philosophical and Technical Essay on Mystery Stories*. Bloomington and London: Indiana University Press, 1977.

Craig, Patricia, and Codagan, Mary. *The Lady Investigates: Women Detectives and Spies in Fiction*. New York: St. Martin's Press, 1981.

Grossvogel, David I. *Mystery and Its Fictions: From Oedipus to Agatha Christie*. Baltimore and London: John's Hopkins University Press, 1979.

Hart, Anne. *The Life and Times of Miss Jane Marple*. New York: Dodd, Mead, 1985.

———. *Agatha Christie's Poirot*. London: Pavipion, 1990.

Haycraft, Howard, ed. *The Art of the Mystery Story*. New York: Grosset and Dunlap, 1946.

Huhn, Peter. "The Detective as Reader: Narrativity and Reading Concepts in Detective Fiction." *Modern Fiction Studies* 33, no. 3 (Fall 1987).

Keating, H. R. F., ed. *Agatha Christie: First Lady of Crime*. New York: Holt, Rinehart and Winston, 1977.

Klein, Kathleen Gregory. *The Woman Detective: Gender and Genre*. Chicago: University of Illinois Press, 1988.

Lambert, Gavin. *The Dangerous Edge*. New York: Grossman Publishers, 1976.

Lehman, David. *The Perfect Murder: A Study in Detection*. New York: The Free Press, 1989.

Mallowan, Max. *Mallowan's Memoirs*. New York: Dodd, Mead, 1977.

Mann, Jessica. *Deadlier than the Male: Why Are Respectable Women So Good at Murder?* New York: Macmillan, 1981.

Masters, Anthony. Literary Agents: *The Novelist as Spy*. New York: Basil Blackwell, 1987.

Moers, Ellen. *Literary Women: The Great Writers*. New York: Anchor Doubleday, 1977.

Morgan, Janet. *Agatha Christie: A Biography*. New York: Knopf, 1984.

Murdoch, Derrick. *The Agatha Christie Mystery*. Toronto: Pagurian Press, 1976.

Nevins, Francis M., Jr., ed. *The Mystery Writers Art*. Bowling Green, Ohio: Bowling Green University Popular Press, 1970.

Osborne, Charles. *The Life and Crimes of Agatha Christie*. New York: Holt, Rinehart, and Winston, 1982.

Ousby, Ian. *Bloodhounds of Heaven: The Detective in English Fiction from Godwin to Doyle*. Cambridge, Mass.: Harvard University Press, 1976.

Peterson, Audrey. *Victorian Masters of Mystery from Wilkie Collins to Conan Doyle*. New York: Frederick Ungar, 1984.

Poovey, Mary. *The Proper Lady and the Woman Writer*. Chicago: University of Chicago Press, 1984.

Ramsey, G. C. *Agatha Christie: Mistress of Mystery*. New York: Dodd, Mead, 1967.

Reddy, Maureen T. *Sisters in Crime: Feminism and the Crime Novel*. New York: Continuum, 1988.

Riley, Dick, and Pam McAllister, eds. *The Bedside, Bathtub, and Armchair Companion to Agatha Christie*. New York: Frederick Ungar, 1979.

Riviere, Francois. *Agatha Christie: Duchesse de la mort*. Paris: Seuil, 1981.

Robyns, Gwen. *The Mystery of Agatha Christie*. New York: Doubleday and Company, 1978.

Ryan, Richard T. *Agatha Christie Trivia*. Boston: Quinlan Press, 1987.

Spacks, Patricia Mayer. *The Female Imagination*. New York: Avon Books, 1972.

Steinbrunner, Chris, and Otto Penzler. *Encyclopedia of Mystery Fiction*. New York: Harcourt Brace Jovanovich, 1976.

Symons, Julian. *Mortal Consequences: A History. From the Detective Story to the Crime Novel*. New York: Harper & Row, 1972.

Symons, Julian, with Tom Adams. *Agatha Christie: the Art of her Crimes: The Paintings of Tom Adams*. New York: Everest House, 1981.

———. *Great Detectives: Seven Original Investigations*. New York: Harry N. Abrams, 1981.

Tynan, Kathleen. *Agatha*. New York: Ballantine Books, 1978.

Wagoner, Mary S. *Agatha Christie*. Boston: G. K. Hall, 1986.

Watson, Colin. *Snobbery with Violence: Crime Stories and their Audiences*. New York: St. Martin's Press, 1971.

Winn, Dilys. *Murderess Ink: The Better Half of the Mystery*. New York: Workman Publishing, 1979.

Acknowledgments

"The Career of Agatha Christie Mallowan" by G. C. Ramsey. From *Agatha Christie: Mistress of Mystery*, by G. C. Ramsey. © 1967 by Dodd, Mead & Company. Reprinted with permission.

"The Case of the Escalating Sales" by Elizabeth Walter. From *Agatha Christie: First Lady of Crime*, edited by H.R.F. Keating. © 1977 by Holt, Rinehart and Winston. Reprinted with permission.

"The Christie Nobody Knew" by Dorothy B. Hughes. From *Agatha Christie: First Lady of Crime*, edited by H.R.F. Keating. © 1977 by Holt, Rinehart and Winston. Reprinted with permission.

"Growing Up" by Agatha Christie. From *An Autobiography* by Agatha Christie. © 1977 by Dodd, Mead & Company. Reprinted with permission.

"Foreword: A Portrait of Agatha Christie" by Julian Symons. From *The New Bedside, Bathtub & Armchair Companion to Agatha Christie*, edited by Dick Riley and Pam McAllister. © 1979 by Ungar Publishing Company. Reprinted with permission.

"The Impact of Gender on Agatha and Her Craft" by Pam McAllister. From *The New Bedside, Bathtub & Armchair Companion to Agatha Christie*, edited by Dick Riley and Pam McAllister. © 1979 by Ungar Publishing Company. Reprinted with permission.

"Counsel for the Defense" by Robert Barnard. From *A Talent to Deceive: An Appreciation of Agatha Christie* by Robert Barnard. © 1980 by Dodd, Mead & Company. Reprinted with permission.

"Appearance and Disappearance" by Charles Osborne. From *The Life and Crimes of Agatha Christie* by Charles Osborne. © 1982 by Holt, Rinehart and Winston. Reprinted with permission.

"Afterward: The Secret of Success" by Gillian Gill. From *Agatha Christie: The Woman and Her Mysteries* by Gillian Gill. © 1990 by The Free Press. Reprinted with permission.

"The Curtain Rises" by Anne Hart. From *The Life and Times of Hercule Poirot*, by Anne Hart. © 1990 by G.P. Putnam's Sons. Reprinted with permission.

Index